Sandy Rodgers

ALL MY MEN
By Sandy Rodgers
Library of Congress Catalog Card Number: 1-040-438
ISBN: 9780972353601

Copyright 2002 Sandy Rodgers
Second Printing: 2005

Please address inquiries to:

Sandy Rodgers
P.O. Box 67
Austell, GA 30168

Edited by
Anne-Marie Drake
Brenda Bennett
Rev. Susan Dalton

Cover Design by
Doing80.com

Testimonials and Recommendations

What people are saying…

"If I were to die today, my obituary has already been written. Your story describes my life completely. It is a light that shines like a million stars, so brightly everyone can see it."

AK- Anthony King, Author, Recording Artist and Actor, Las Vegas, NV

"Thank you for your book. You have known some incredible men in your life. It should be required reading for all feminists and man-haters because you give relationships with the opposite sex a powerful spin."

Albert Clayton Gaulden, Author and Founder The Sedona Intensive, Sedona, AZ

"Your topics deal with the most personal issues that we live with daily. I was inspired."

J.T. Brayboy, President, Atlanta Chapter of National Association of Black Narcotic Agents, Atlanta, GA

"It was evident you dedicated a lot of time and hard work to this project, and it will prove beneficial to others."

Bernadine Brown, Principal/CEO, IMANI Associates Consulting, Inc., Atlanta, GA

"You are a woman of God and that is demonstrated in your past and present actions. The message you bring is a learning

experience for all ages, a message of hope and action. You are a builder of churches (the human heart)."

Pastor Gloria Bennett, Marietta Chapel Church in Marietta, GA

"I have always expected great things from you and you are still proving me right. Your book is an excellent narrative of what people can accomplish when their motives are clear and loving."

George McKenna, Area Superintendent, Pasadena City Schools, Pasadena CA

"After reading your book, my sister and I, both in our sixties began a dialogue about the positive male role models in our lives. It took 'All My Men' to bring us sisters closer than we have ever been. Thank you for your words of encouragement and love."

Delora Holmon, East St. Louis, MO

"Reading "All My Men" just reminded me of my family. Names may be different, characters the same however, so many stories were similar to my own family. It was like reading about my own life and family."

Cornelius Butler, Atlanta GA.

"The book made me cry. I had been ignoring the hurt that the absence of my father in my life caused. I forgot just how much I hurt. I cried because I have been married to a wonderful woman for many years and could not tell her I loved her. After reading the book

and speaking with Sandy, I am now free to express my love for my wife and my father!"

Roosevelt Deal Jr., LeCompte LA

ALL MY MEN...

This book is dedicated to all the men in my life, both past and present. My love story dedicated to you.

To the men whose blood I share.

To the men who taught me along the way about life and living, struggle and survival, fun, sharing, tenderness and harshness. LOVE. Men who were sometimes afraid to love, that did not understand how to love, men that felt abandoned and alone.

To the men that have stuck with me through the thick and thin of times.

To all these men I give honor because of their unconditional love, I salute you for allowing me to see you in your true essence.

To the men that are not mentioned, not because I forgot your name or how you influenced my life, just know I love you also!

To the women who gave birth to these men and to the women that have loved them I say thank you.

God, I thank you for blessing me with each man mentioned and those that are not mentioned. Thank you for allowing my life to be enriched by every man I know.

This book is written to honor ALL the men I have ever known in any capacity, at any point in my life. This is a true LOVE story. I have accepted that everything that was shared was LOVE. To me that means its all good! This is a book dedicated to healing;

the pains, the lies, the myths and the destruction that has been passed down.

I share my memories of those that remain in spirit because their physical bodies are no longer with us. I speak of my family men that support and encourage me. All my sons, although I only gave birth to one, I have numerous adopted sons. The Spiritual Teachers who I cherish for sharing the truth of God with me; my work comrades that always seemed to have a little story to tell me; my little men, my grandson who amazes me and keeps me young and growing daily, my nephews who just love their Auntie. And lastly without hesitation I share my romantic encounters. Most folks don't understand me when I say I love each of these men still. They look at me in wonder and that's okay too. Perhaps I am helping them to heal, if pain exists for them with past relationships.

Ultimately, this is a book of and for healing. Love is the only healing power in the Universe. This is my love story of the major men in my life.

My Inspiration

The year 2002 has indeed been an awesome year.

God has gifted me with all the support, motivation and encouragement I required for this project, in human form. There has been so many who have inspired me, challenged me (sometimes the person may not have recognized just how they blessed me) to let my creative genius flow to brighten and help others.

Each of the ministers at my place of worship, Hillside Chapel and Truth Center in Atlanta, Georgia, have contributed significantly to this writing. As well as my brother, William Saafir and my Daddy.

Rev. Dr. Barbara Lewis King: Founder-Minister of Hillside Chapel and Truth Center Inc. is my spiritual Mother and teacher of life. To know Dr. Barbara is to know unequivocally she will challenge you to bring out the very best, your God-self to share with all of humanity. I simply love and admire this Beautiful Soul because she realizes we each, to some degree, harbor restrictions we have placed on ourselves. With Dr. Barbara you just simply cannot or will not remain constant or stagnant. A person must be willing to grow in their acceptance of Truth. Dr. Barbara not only teaches and preaches Truth, she lives it and shares on a very human level her experiences. There is no mysticism or magic just Truth. Each time she looks me directly in the eye I feel compelled to deliver my best to the Universe. This is but one gift, God has chosen me to be effectively multi-talented. But those gifts could still be laying dormant if it wasn't for the impeccable leadership of this Prayed-up, Spirit-filled, Awesome, Beautiful Spirit. I love you, Dr. Barbara for teaching me about Divine-birthright, staying in recovery, staying on course, agree with Spiritual blessings, allow my light to shine brightly and my supply cannot be withheld.

Rev. Gertrude Moore: A bright smile always welcoming my presence. Her enduring sweetness, even as she was faced with challenges in her own family. Rev. Gertrude says "Never give up on God". Although my goal is to stay focused and centered sometimes I may falter. And it's at that very moment that the inspirational message 'never give up on God' floats gently from the lips of this powerful spirit.

Rev. Susan Dalton: Rev. Dalton has been my strength when I was new on my discovery path. From facilitating a support group to serving as the assistant of Church Affairs – a title I've conceived- she literally runs the daily operations. Regardless of the position, she has been a pillar of positive strength; coaching me when I chose inappropriate words to describe my challenges to remaining ever supportive of my actions. Rev. Susan, you will probably never fully understand the positive impact you have been in my life. I love you so much.

Rev. Rocco Errico, Dean of Biblical Studies: My initial class with Rev. Rocco was 'Genesis, the Mysteries of Creation'. In Divine time I was able to complete the full series on Genesis. I had questions from my childhood concerning 'the beginning' with simplicity and Near Eastern knowledge Rev. Rocco answered and made the story clear and acceptable for me. The joy of the Lord is your strength' is all that he said to me in a healing service. That released me from the limitations and seriousness I had placed on situations in my life. I began to experience more joy, more laughter, more freedom; more permission to keep going without the extra, unnecessary weight of worry. Thanks Rev. Rocco.

Rev. Robert Kilgore is a remarkably joyous and joy-filled spirit. Being in Rev. Kilgore's presence is pure motivation.
One desires to report their progress on the path to knowing, it's his persona, his aura, his full acceptance that drives you.
His smile lights up the world. He shares openly with everyone who seeks his counsel. Rev. Kilgore, I appreciate your kindness and support, your strength and gentleness. When I grow up I want to be just like you! I love you.

Rev. Darin Woodard: This young brother is a powerhouse in the Pulpit. I have just recently received the opportunity to hear his sermons. "Revealing God" was one powerful sermon. Rev. Darrin spoke directly to me "Reveal God in all you do", "My specialness shines through" and "Pull the weeds up form the root so they don't return". I majored in Journalism in 1968 at U.C. Irvine, knew I loved writing thirty four years ago. Thanks Darrin I'm revealing my God-power to the Universe. Rev. Darrin talked about eradicating false beliefs from ones consciousness "It is done unto us as we believe". And "Let my light shine – each has a calling, a ministry to fulfill. We each have a special gift to contribute to the positive-ness of humankind" This is my gift! What's the question? I love you Rev. Darrin.

Rev. Dolores Jackson is always glowing like an angel. Without a lot of dialog between us, Rev. Dolores has demonstrated her unquestionable belief in me and my abilities. I just see it in her eyes and hear it when she speaks of me. Rev. Dolores you have been a constant source of inspiration and I thank you. I am so grateful for your presence in my life.

My brother, **William Saafir**, and I ended 2001 exploring the social unrest globally. Leading into 2002 we share a vision of what we are calling a 'Universal Spiritual Movement'. We are affiliated with different religious doctrines but each a sincere TRUTH student. We have acknowledged this awakening, this power-filled movement in people we know, in the workplace and across varying doctrines. We embrace it lovingly and have accepted our roles in bringing this movement to fruition. William is conducting seminars and developing the establishment of a self-contained/governed community based solely on Truth, the teachings of God. There are new arenas opening for both of us. As they open we remain steadfastly supportive of each other. We have knocked and the doors are being opened. We have diligently sought (asked), we are being blessed bountifully. William remains a sincere servant, seeking and sharing Truth in all that he does. He has lifted me up to this higher level of acceptance and I am thankful. William, your inspiration keeps me going when I want to stop, Thank You.

My Daddy, **James Armstead**, has been at my side from the very conception of this book.

His presence felt from the first page to the last and everything in between. His admiration of my writing ability, unyielding support to accomplishing my goals to reminding me to get some rest! All has been received by me, his baby girl, with sincere gratitude. These have been the major players for this undertaking. Each have aided me as only they could. I am so grateful to be blessed with them and the many other well wishers who knew I was writing a book and cheered me all along the way.

Preface

Man is a thinking being. In fact, he did not really become a true human being until he developed as an intellect. It is through the intellect that he ponders, reflects and imagines. This marvelous imagination sets him apart from all the rest of creation, not to mention his ability to look back on what he has done in the past and improve upon it. Man is so amazing that his mind can literally travel to the edge of the universe, reverse its direction, and then travel inward into the mysterious world of the atom.

Just think: the mind of man can accomplish the amazing feat of encompassing the whole of human history! Even more awesome, he has been given the potential to identify the contents of everything in creation. Exercising this ability the human mind expands and develops until it rises to the highest of the high, even higher than the angels, and becomes the 'crown of creation'. Unfortunately, man can also fall to become the lowest of the low, if he fails to use this gift properly.

A wonderful creation is this creature called man. This wonderful creature has gained, by the Grace of G-d, mastery of his environment. From the bottom of the deepest ocean to the top of the highest mountain, man has applied his intellect and extracted knowledge to guide him in his quest for the expression of his G-d given excellence.

As great as man has become, the true mind recognizes that the one who created all that exists is always much, much greater. Man, being true to the best of his rational thinking processes, focuses on the Greater for unlimited development of his intellect. He recognizes that he needs help to make the journey of life successful; help not just from creation, but also, more importantly from the Creator. Who can give better help than the one who created all that exists, including us, from nothing?

At the very foundation of intellectual growth and human progress is the healthy use of the five senses. These five senses, given proper expression, will lead us to higher and higher refinement. Ultimately, with time and plenty of help, the human being evolves to become a very highly sensitive creature.

The highest expression of these sensitivities is that of love. Love is the well from which all other sensitivities spring forth. Love is the purest of all human expressions. Evidence of this purity is the fact that you have to love a thing before you can give your whole mind (your whole self) to it. It is this unselfish, unrestrained giving of yourself to the things you value that allows your excellence to manifest itself.

In the West, the expression of love, outside of a sexual context, in most social circles is taboo for men. This expression of love is generally not at all considered a very masculine trait. The macho, false masculine, role that is heavily promoted in the society, is a trap that confuses the sensitivities of men. It has little, if anything at all, to do with tenderness or kindness. This very image robs men of the opportunity to be truly human. Ironically, this self-defeating artificial development in the mind of men has actually stunted the masculine growth of far too many men.

Any time a father has to wrestle with his emotions and force himself to hug his own teenage or adult son, something is seriously wrong. While that is bad enough, it is often even more difficult for a father to tell his older son that he loves him, even though he loves him very much. This emotional tug of war causes deep-seated psychological problems for the father and the son. To top it all off, the worst part of this problem is that it has the tendency to repeat itself.

This might sound like some remote, detached analysis, but I assure you it is not. It is real for me as, I am sure, it is for the majority of men infected with this malady of the western mind. This diseased mindset inhibits the healthy growth of one of our most precious assets: human sensitivity. Without a caring heart our sensibilities are blinded. When the sensibilities are blinded full expression of the human potential becomes virtually impossible.

We are at the door of an unleashing of the human mind and spirit that humanity has not experienced since the renaissance. Global man is taking front stage as he did at the beginning of human history. In order to push back the artificial barriers in the human mind we must return to a pure sense of the unity of mankind. That can only be accomplished if man opens his human heart to other men, as it was intended in the beginning.

Man's evolved role is that of the legs or the support of the society. To carry the society forward we must have the heart and the mind of the 'real' man. To be giants in our social life we must first be giants in our emotional or spiritual life.

A man must be able to be kind and tender hearted and not lose sight of the fact that he is a man, not a woman. A man must be able to have feelings for babies, the elderly, the environment, the weak, the oppressed and his own son. A man must be able to express his love for his fellow man without feeling that he is anything less than a man. As a matter of fact, he should feel even stronger as a 'real' man when he expresses that love for his human brother.

Although, the heart is not the boss in our life, it serves as the driving force and the mellowing agent for the boss. The boss of the human life is the intellect. The mind takes charge, directs and gives substance to the human life.

The misunderstanding of the role of the heart creates havoc in our lives. The human heart motivates, stimulates, sensitizes and energizes the life. It is not equipped to order our life. Nor is it equipped to give understanding and mastery neither of self nor of our environment. The job of self-mastery, as well as, maintaining and utilizing the environment is the job of the boss: the human mind.

Western man has denied himself full expression as a human being not understanding the delicate balance between human sensitivity and the human intellect. Our earthly paradise reflects this balance and this full expression of the human potential, 'All My Men' is a very personal account of the life of a very sensitive human being. Full of love for the Creator of all things and for the humanity that He created, nothing is spared in this inspiring demonstration of the healing power of love in our life. In the words of the most perfect of all human beings: "You will not enter paradise unless you have faith, and you will not attain to faith unless you first love you one another."

William Saafir

How It Began

So much time and negative energy is lost by bashing the Black man and blaming the White man for all the injustices in our society. Both have helped me to learn about life, living, love and the pursuit of happiness. There is no bitterness in my heart or thoughts, just the same unconditional love that has been extended and shared with me. I now understand and fully accept the men that could not demonstrate love perhaps did not know how to express themselves. Perhaps the weight of the pain they had experienced along life's journey forced them to place a shield around their innermost feelings. Protection of their heart was their only defense and/or survival. I cannot and will not attempt to speak for them. My desire is to only share the best of these men as only I know it.

Many spoke to me in ways they were not able to do with others, particularly the ones closest to them such as wives or lovers. Perhaps the reason is that I listened, truly listened to what they had to say with an open heart and mind. The saying goes we have one mouth and two ears and we should govern ourselves accordingly. In other words listen twice as much as we talk. So this is what I did, not even knowing what the law was. This is what prompted me to consider organizing a Men's Ministry. The letter on the following page is the one I sent out and some of the replies I received.

November 14, 1996 (incidentally my mother's birthday)

Dear,

I have been whispered to from GOD, prompted by SPIRIT and asked by several Black Men to take a more active role in ministering, to helping to empower Black Men. These men say I have been an exceptionally positive influence in their lives. I accept and acknowledge I have a special gift/talent to be open, honest and supportive of Black Men mainly because I love you unconditionally. Although I do not know what the final outcome will look like, be it a book, seminars or something else, I am going forward with this vision.

YOU came to my mind because of the bond we have and a very important part of your life was shared with me. I am asking for your prayers and also for any ideas you may have regarding this vision of mine. To help and support me in this undertaking, please take some time to explore how I have affected or influenced you along your journey in life. Please write your response and forward to me at the above address.

Thanks for loving and supporting me in return. Knowing me as only you can, please provide me with any additional wisdom or insights you care to share with me. Feel free to include any personal information, such as your age, occupation, martial status, relationship to me, etc., you think is relevant to this project. Thanks for taking the time to reply.

I anxiously await your reply. I LOVE YOU…….

This first letter is from a former modeling
student, **Quincy Brown.**

Dearest Sandy,

*HEY!!! I would ask how you are doing but as
I can see you are doing very well!!! I am so
proud of YOU! You Go Girl! The vision that
you have is nothing new to me. You do have a
special gift and I'm glad you thought enough
of me to contact me for my input/ideas. I
wish I could be there in Atlanta when you
start your new Modeling Company because I
really miss modeling. I haven't modeled
since I was at Nu Vision. It seems I can't
find any modeling companies and the couple I
did see had a catch to modeling with them.*

*First I want to thank you for the honesty
you've shown me through your own actions. I
remember what happened with the
"International Gold" contest. I think that
was the theme and I believe it was the one
where —(name withheld) was supposed to be
handling the financial prize packages and
somehow the finances weren't together like
they should have been. Anyway, I saw how
honest you were and how it really upset you
that somebody didn't do what they were
supposed to do to make the whole contest the
success it was suppose to be. Just by the
fact alone that you were one of 2 other
people who started Nu Vision shows me that
you are a woman of vision which is the first
idea I have to share with you in your
endeavor.*

*The first step to empowering Black Men is to
help them first find the vision in their
life. Every man needs to have a vision
of how he sees himself and how others see
him, also he needs to have a vision of where*

he sees himself going. Whether it be
financially, emotionally, physically,
mentally or whatever. I can't think of where
it is in the Bible but, the Bible says:
"Without vision, the people perish" or
something to that effect. So first Black Men
must somehow envision what they want to see
in and of themselves.

The second step to empowering Black Men is
showing them that once they have a vision
what steps they will need to take to make
that vision a reality. It's a known fact
that girls mature faster than boys,
therefore it will take some men longer than
others to see what steps they will need to
take and for other men Sandy you will have
to break it down to them step-by-step. Some
men you come in contact with will already
have a vision but will need to find out what
steps or what actions they will need to take
to reach their goal. When I was attending
Long Beach State University they had a
computer program that helped you decide on
what you wanted to be or what type of career
you needed to get into. I don't know if
there is a computer program out there on the
market that you can use or if you can't find
one, let me know and I will try to create
one that you can use in this endeavor.

The third and last step to empowering Black
Men is that Sandy a lot of men you come in
contact with will need love, understanding
and encouragement. All qualities of which
you possess and have demonstrated. In fact
I'm sure that is the reason why those men
you've touched are telling you to take a
more active role to empowering other Black
Men. Sandy, you know as well as I know that
quite a few Black Men have made terrible
decisions in life such as having babies and

not being there to take care of them,
selling drugs, stealing, using drugs, being
abusive to their families as well as to
themselves, going in and out of jail, and
the list goes on and on. However, when they
come to you after they've finally awaken and
want to change their life, these men will
need someone strong and positive to stand by
them when other close friends don't believe
they've changed and want to abandon their
friendship. Therefore, they will need a
support group. They'll need to know without
a doubt that somebody really cares and still
loves them. That would be a good time to
introduce Christ to them and to show them
His love and share with them about salvation
or at least that Jesus is real. They will
need some type of spiritual guidance, and if
they don't want to receive that, then at
least their support group will be there for
them.

The task that you are undertaking is one
that you were doing back when I met you in
1988 at Ubitquitdus. The only difference is
that you will be in charge instead of
someone else. (name withheld) had this same
idea, but (as most men you are going to come
in contact with) he lost sight of his goal
and let other things on his mind detour him
and blind-side him into the ditch he fell
in. Sandy, don't you make the same mistakes
as he did. You keep Jesus first in your
life, above family, friends and career
because if your whole world fell apart no
one, not one person will stand by your side
through the storm like Jesus. You keep your
goal, dreams and your purpose in front of
you. Never loose sight of your purpose and
you'll reach your goal. Sandy, be prepared
to be let down and disappointed by some of
the Black Men you may help. Some of them

won't want to hear encouragement and guidance from a woman, others you help won't even say "Thank you" and others won't really be serious about trying to change their life so it will seem like a waste of time trying to help them, but, just remember that if you can help just one Black Man find his way on the right road, then you've reached your goal.

As for myself, I am 27 and I'm single with no kids (thank God). I am a student at Computer Learning Center and I am now affluent with Microsoft Word, Excel, and Access. Word is a professional word processing program, Excel is an accounting program and Access is a database program which in short is like having a Pacific Bell customer list with how much each customer owes, has paid, what features they have and all sorts of things like that. It manages large amounts of data in simple direct ways. I type 60 words per minute and the school is supposed to find me a job when I graduate in January 1997. Since I've learned so much there I could teach all 3 programs myself. I have a vision of being financially independent and how I want to do it is through investments and such. But first I need a good job so I can set some money aside to invest with and once I set enough aside I can turn my vision into a reality. I'm praying for you, I love you and wish you much success in all your endeavors. Let me know how everything turns out and if I can be of anymore assistance to you. These were just a few ideas I thought of to help.

Talk with you soon. I Love You and am Proud of You…….

The next response is from my cousin/brother,
a person who has graciously stuck with me
through it ALL.

Dear Sandy,

*First of all let me say I was very elated to
hear from you. I am really glad that things
are beginning to turn in a positive manner
and your outlook on life has been renewed. I
am writing this letter on my one year
anniversary of becoming a member of
Alcoholics Anonymous, and I too can attest
to a change in life and a renewed Spiritual
growth. I was pondering what I could say or
write to help you in your endeavor and I am
going to focus only on conversations that
took place while both of us were going thru
difficult times in our lives. I can remember
when going thru my divorce I would seek out
any and everybody that would listen to me.
Our conversations were always of a positive
nature and you would always let me vent my
anger and frustrations before you would
speak. What I am saying is that (listening)
is one of the aspects that I can see that
you have because a lot of people would say I
don't have time or I don't want to get
involved. Responses and reactions are very
important when a person is in trouble either
mentally or physically and is seeking help
or advice. Your responses would always leave
me with some sort of sense of direction. I
knew deep down within what I needed to do
but facing up to it was hard. You let me
know that as far as being a good parent and
husband I did my part and it was time for me
to focus on myself and Stephfan because no
amount of effort could resolve my other
problem. So the second thing that I would
say is that your responses are direct and to
the point whether a person wants to hear*

*them or not. Finally, you told me that I
must put all of my troubles and problems in
the hand of someone that has all power. For
me that wasn't easy to do because I believed
in God but I really didn't have Faith. Once
I finally got that perspective in order I
was able to move on. So, finally I would say
that you let me know that Prayer and belief
in God is the key. I have had many stumbling
blocks in life as with my alcoholism and I
have found out that God will remove things
from our lives that we think are
uncontrollable. I don't know if this will
help you or not but for me this is what I
know you did for me. May God Bless you and
keep you and if I can be of further
assistance to you let me know.*

Love, **Glenn**
Mission in Life is to be happy, joyous and
free. And to help others the way others have
helped me (smile)

This next letter is from my brother,
William, my rock of Gibraltar.

Sandy,

*May God Bless you in the unfolding of a
particular role that you have in the
uplifting of the African-American people.
We all have a unique contribution to make in
the rise of our people in becoming a very
productive member of the human family, as an
ethnic group. I pray that God gives you the
wherewithal to blossom into your uniqueness.*

*I feel a special closeness to you, not just
because I am your brother, but rather
because of the sensitivity, the untiring
support and the deeply rooted responsiveness
that you have demonstrated time and time*

again. It's the womanness in you that, when shared, brings out the best in men. God designed it that way. As a matter of fact, God's prophet said that "paradise lies at the foot of the mother".

Stay strong. Keep true to the nature that God has placed in you and you will continue to be a force for bringing out the best in the African-American man, or in any human being, for that matter, regardless of gender or ethnic group.

Your Brother and fellow Servant of God, William Saafir

And the last is from one of my adopted God-Sons, Bobby Shelton.

Hey Sandy,

What's up? I'm very happy that you're doing so well. Sorry it took me so long to respond to your letter. I have no excuse. Well, I'll just continue to type and something useful will come to my fingertips. (that's the plan anyway). In my mind, when I think of you I remember how creative you have always been. Even when I was in high school, your house was always different and unique. This is something I think we have in common: the need to be creative.

My ultimate need and want is to make my living creating something. There are those, some even in my family that have pursued and are pursuing the activity of making money for the sake of making money. They have talked to me about their vast wealth. Don't get me wrong, I respect them for their achievements, but to me the real trick will be to make money creating things for people, artistically. Not just to mimic what someone else did to make money.

It's not enough, for me, to make it off of some white man's idea. I'm not prejudice, but logic tells me that the insurance business, for example, has been here a long time and a white person thought it up. Going out everyday to make people sign up and write a check to get so and so insurance policy is not how I want to spend my time, even if there's good money in it, that's not what my life is for.

My move to East St. Louis has helped me to see that I am a creator not a mimicker. I've spent a large portion of my life doing what I called "pursuing a music career". Now, I think that I was learning how to make something of value from scratch and how to "bring ideas to life". A song or a music production starts as an idea. Then there are the steps you take to bring it to life. It takes other people to help. It's like a concert of people and their skill all adding to the pot, under the direction of the director.

Anyway, I am now in the printing, graphic design and information business. I think of it as the perfect next step. Now I organize "concerts of people and their skill adding to the pot" of visual creations instead of audio creations. But this pursuit does not rely as much on luck and nepotism as the music business. And this pursuit has a front row seat in the future of American business. We are now in the Information Age. Music is information too, but it's a lot harder to get in the door of the music business than it is to get into this thing I'm doing now.

And I am creating! A customer asks me to make them a business card...I ask them about their business...then I go to my computer and software and create a business card for them and personalize it to their particular needs with pictures and typestyles that "say" that person or business. My company is called Tailor-Maid Typing & Design.

I'm even working on a book with a guy who has epilepsy. The book is about living with epilepsy. He is not the best writer, so he just gives me his notes every week and I organize them into book form.

In your letter you mentioned the word "book" and I thought, "I would love to write a book with her, in any capacity." I don't know if you have a computer system yet but I do. I have a computer, printing, faxing, I'm even on the internet. So it is not necessary for us to be in the same city to work together.

This leads me back to the matter at hand: What do we as young Black Americans need for success in the future. Technology! But I'm not necessarily referring to the floorshow items like portable phones and pagers. No, I'm talking about every Black home having at least a fax machine so that we can send documents to one another. Documents are where it's at. Why you ask? Because verbal agreements and commitments over the phone and at dinner are not enough. They are like ideas. They have to be turned into something tangible before they can go anywhere. A piece of paper with an idea or plan written on it is something tangible.

Once an idea or plan is on paper and is sent via fax or internet to others, a seed is now planted and it has form...either words on paper or on a disk or on a computer's hard drive. It can be referred to again anytime it is picked up and read. What else?

All black men need to understand on some level about the current trend of decentralization. They need to know that they are becoming a man during a transitional period in America, from large corporations hiring you and taking care of your future to a world where you are better off working for yourself or acquiring skills that has a place in this information era. Some of them just think that there are no jobs for the Black Man, and leave it at that. And start selling drugs. I submit, that that is an entrepreneurial attitude, now find another product to sell.

What else?

Young Black women, stop thinking the old fashioned way with regards to the myth of "having babies to keep your man". Don't no man who ain't got a job or a plan for a bright future need no babies. And if you do this country shit to keep your man, one of two things may happen: He is going to leave you, in which case you will be forced into a life where you are no longer the VIP, you will be working for your kids with no assistance (I'm not saying that's bad just be aware that it usually happens) or, he is going to stay with you, lose what few ideas he may have had for a bright future, become a night security guard, start drinking too much, and unfortunately start having the impulse to kick your ass every now and then for having those damn babies in the first place. You didn't inseminate yourself, but he'll forget about that as he's slapping your ass in the face and drunk.

Sorry, Sandy, sometimes I fly off the handle on that subject.

My cousin is currently caught up in the Baby trap. He's a baby himself, his girlfriend is from a welfare family and has the negative welfare mentality. So to her, keeping my cousin is like winning the lottery or getting food stamps or an increase in welfare money. She can't see past that. She gave birth to his daughter about a year ago. To give you an example of what I'm saying, they were living together, and he put her out for being lazy. You know the scenario…he comes home from a hard days work and she hasn't cooked nothin' up in the place. Not a French fry. Not a ham sandwich. Haven't even cleaned up the apartment. And she was letting other guys call there and talk to her on the phone trying to hook up with her. So he put her out.

About 2 months later, he let her come back. Why? He told me that he felt sorry for her. She had no place else to go. I mean no problems were resolved between the couple nothing discussed, he just felt sorry for her. Before long, guess what? She announced that she was pregnant again. I guess she figures if one baby doesn't work, two should do it. From what I was told, she almost died during her last pregnancy and delivery and the baby had birth defects. But in her mind, this is what she has to do. Sad isn't it?

Lets move on.

Parents have to let go of some old fashioned ideas. Most lower and middle class parents are only satisfied fully when their son or daughter gets a good job with a big company.

Some others are elated after their son or daughter becomes successful in their own business or becomes a great athlete or Artist. But very few support new progressive business ideas in the early stages. I know people who's parents would shell out $85,000.00 or more for their son or daughter to go to college but won't give $100.00 for a good business idea. Less than half of that $85k could launch a good business idea into existence with style and class. Don't get me wrong, it has to be a good idea first. So parents, stay open minded. Remember the world is made up of people who sell things and people who buy things. And everybody who is anybody is getting paid by the people who buy things. Not the other way around…think about it. The salesman and the business owners are the financially rich. Even the doctors are in business….the business of people's health. People will hand you their hard earned money if you can offer them something of value.

One of the best feelings I get occurs every time a customer hands me money and I put it in my pocket and I know that I don't have to pay it back or anything because I earned it. Or if I see that I have a high phone bill any particular month, I can generate money just by doing a mail out to my existing customers offering them a discount coupon or something, and it never fails, I get a few calls for printing orders.

So parents at least listen to and think about you son or daughter's idea before dismissing it.

O.K. Sandy, I'll stop for now.
Love,
Bobby

As you can see from the various letters and responses I received the men in my life come from all backgrounds. All have their own particular contribution to add value to my life and yours. But one must listen to hear the wisdom and insights from each soul that delivers a message to us. We cannot prejudge what the person is saying for it is valid for that person and their experience. We can learn a great deal about life by listening, and what my brothers are telling me is that I do that quite well. Thank you Brothers, I accept your generous compliments.

This book comes five years after writing this. Be assured it comes in the most timely manner possible. I have grown so much in LOVE, have released so much pain. Have made a conscious decision to only love. And it was not always an easy task, I was simply sick and tired of hurting. I knew I had the power to change and I did!

My heart has been touched so many times by the sensitivity of the men I now write about. Some caused what I called, labeled pain before I understood and decided to look at the lessons differently. There is undoubtedly confusion, unmet dreams, an inability to express the deepest thoughts and feelings we have. This I believe is the root cause of my having to somehow place blame on someone else to justify my own pain and lack of understanding.

We can look for goodness or stay stuck in negativity. Ultimately it is our choice and we can move forward in love or remain living in the past, which is a place we cannot change. We can only move forward. Only change our attitude, but only when we look at life with the eyes of love. There is no movement by straddling the fence. We are either on one side or the other. One cannot exist for very long by not taking a stance for what they believe in, again its our choice. We are powerful beings. The only living creatures empowered with free will. Are we/you/me freed by the tender actions of love or enslaved by the negative feelings that drain life right out of us? Love and choosing love is the single most healing thing we can do, that's absolutely free of charge, to improve one's life, health and happiness. It does not make you weak or subordinate. It empowers you to live a full rich life, right here on earth. So to that end I have chosen love. To love what has not appeared as love in the past. To love the present and all that is in it. To love the future and all of its possibilities.

Men are the back bone of this society. Men are the fathers of humanity. Men are the necessary elements in conceiving life. Men represent strength. Men are the providers. We must love our men if we are to truly love ourselves. There is no separation. Just as the creation of life involves both the male and female, so does the existence of mankind, humankind requires both the male and female energy to survive.

I ask you to freely choose love in all your interactions with others. Pay particular attention to our men, of all races, whom we sometimes choose to barter our love with. Women must first love each other as well as our men. And men must do the same thing, and choose to love the women in return. When love is the key element in human relationships and interactions, a better society erupts with such force that all of

our social ills are completely destroyed!
WOW - what a vision to behold!

My childhood was rather typical, raised in a
typical family. The unspoken yet often
yelled phrases from the elder women in the
community all but destroyed the image of
strong men, especially Black men. Was told
not to expect much from them lest I be
disappointed, don't put too much of myself
in a relationship because men cheat and its
okay because that's just who they are, dogs.
Never trust a man because he will end up
stepping on your heart. Always have an
option - implying don't truly commit to a
man especially a Black man.

Subsequently the majority of my life has
been spent listening to and engaging in
conversations with my sisters, both old
and young, all nationalities, discussing the
awful predicament we found ourselves in. How
we began with a sweet, affectionate
individual only for him to become a 'dog'.
Or we spent years attempting to change them
into the desired man we wanted to share our
lives with. It took decades of this type of
behavior before I fully realized that we
brought or created in our existence that
which we held in our thoughts. And it is
still applicable today. A very dear wise
friend of mine recently described her eight
year marriage, which is now being dissolved,
to man whom she has financially supported
throughout the entire marriage. A man
incapable of expressing affection. This was
being shared with me by a beautiful,
extremely intelligent and talented sister. A
sister who always dated corporate executive
types, or least financially independent men.

A sister who is very compassionate and affectionate to everyone she knows. I was completely caught off guard. As she unleashed that destructive tongue, I listened to the bashing, she needed to rid herself of that built up anger. When she was finished, I shared with her what I had discovered to be truth. I told her to examine her thoughts and motives. What would make her stay in a relationship with a man like she had described? What vision did she hold about herself? Was she going to fix him? Too old to get another man? What? That was difficult for her to hear. In the end she completely understood what I had said to her and decided to change her self-talk and expectations about men and her future.

Ladies we cannot continue to bash our men because we are holding nonsense in our thoughts. Like some of the men in this book, when we begin with a higher level of Self-acceptance, Self-esteem and Self-love we will draw those types of men into our lives. And if by chance we slip, there will be warning signs. All you will need to do is heed to those warnings. Be strong enough to admit it and walk away. Stop trying to fix people. PLEASE!

I am so grateful for being filled with understanding and compassion. I am thankful for being used as vessel of truth. To share with the same sister circle I had once joined in bashing our men to now be able to communicate a different way of thinking and healing.

Listening to the ol' folks wisdom was always hard to hear. You knew they held an awful lot of pain. And they would belittle the men in my life, my uncles, brothers and so on.

This always left me with a bad taste because I knew something different. I remained childlike, knowing there was goodness and love in men and women. I allowed myself to feel their pain and their joys. I allowed myself to feel! After all, most of my male relatives were my heroes.

The Black men I knew and know are all strong, loving, kind, sensitive - at least most of them. And those that are not and were not had been crushed by life and they simply forgot they possessed those qualities.

Men from all walks of life have shared with me. Young men, old men, black men, white men, Asian and Hispanic men, professional men, blue collar and laborers. Family men, career criminals, homosexuals, the corner/neighborhood drunk or wine-o as we called them as kids. All chose to share with me as only they could. They all chose to protect me, in the way they knew how, they all loved me and today that is simply enough to keep me going and loving them in return!

To Those Who
Are Gone and not Forgotten

To those that have gone on before me
and there are many.

All my men, my Grandfathers Papa T-Boy
and Papa Hawk; my step father Odis Brown; My
brother Rudy Odis Brown; my God fathers Bob
Bailey and Prentice Westbrook; my many
Uncles - Joe, Tot, Gerald, J.D., Ed and Dave
affectionately known as Uncle Grass. There
was always so much love shown, from combing
and scratching up the dandruff with Uncle Ed
to following Uncle Dave and wondering why he
was always cutting someone's grass, thus
the nickname 'Uncle Grass'. From sitting at
Uncle Joe's feet listening intently to his
stories of our history to wondering why
Uncle JD always smoked a cigar and called me
Santa Fe. Like the railway, maybe it was
because he couldn't pronounce my name La
Sandra. To watching Uncle Tot in his Navy
uniform always looking handsome and
debonair. Uncle Gerald and I had a very
special relationship, and his daughters and
wife shared him with me without any hassle.
My God father Bob who until the end I had
problem understanding why he was always
away. Later to discover he spent most of his
life in and out of jail. And Prentice
Westbrook, who I called Puny because of his
size. I was there when he was wasting away
with cancer, he was the first person I saw
that I knew without a doubt he was dying.

My Grandfathers I barely remember other
than, Papa Hawk was always, always smiling
and walking through the little town of
LeCompte Louisiana. I knew, without knowing
him that well that Papa T-Boy was a proud
and accomplished man by anyone's standards.
My step father Odis Brown, who taught me how
to fish, that I later taught both of my
husbands. Odis taught us many things and the

one probably most important was how to be a
business owner, with little formal education
on his part.

Lastly there's my brother Rudy. He was
such a wonder-filled person/Spirit. So let's
visit with each of them as I share my
lessons of love from each of them. This will
not be in particular order, as the person
comes to mind I will write about their
influence on my life.

Let's start however with my younger brother,
Rudy. Rudy died a violent death at much too
early an age. He was struck down and thrown
2 city blocks by a man who was high on the
popular drug of that time, PCP. Even the
violent death did not distract from his
otherwise beautiful life of loving everyone.

Rudy Odis Brown

Rudy was born eight years after me. So that
meant I was the Baby of the family until he
appeared in this world, our family. Well, no
one taught me about jealousy, especially
with my brother. There were times, and most
of my younger years when I could not stand
him. How dare he come along and take away
from my special place in the family! But
that never stopped Rudy from exploring the
world and having as much fun as possible
along the journey. As a baby he got into
more trouble, drinking medicines that
belonged to other family members. Sticking
his fingers into wall sockets. He was a very
active, very curious young boy. He
eventually grew on me, but not until after I
had tried to tip him over in his stroller
skating down the driveway of our house. I
tell you he laughed all the way down that
steep drive way, I had to laugh too! Small
children don't understand sharing the title

role, things were better when our youngest brother was born. Because then neither of us were the Baby any longer. What rationale for a small kid.

Rudy always had time to visit everyone! And he never drove back the same way he traveled to a location. These may sound like little things but it was these very things that people, especially me remember the most about him. His loving, generous Spirit and how he did what he did in his own unique way.

His death was difficult to accept, it literally tore the family apart. He was so young and full of life. My thoughts were, God why didn't you take me instead? I am thankful for Rudy's loving-kindness that he shared with everyone he ever met. His insistence on treating everyone fairly and just. Rudy was extremely sensitive and aware of how to treat people. I believe each person he ever met felt they had a special relationship with him, that was just the way he was. Everyone was different in their uniqueness and he appreciated those qualities.

Rudy was tall in statue, compared to me anyway! Firmly built and loved life. He was kind and considerate to all.

To him I wrote this:
June 10, 1980

Rudy
I miss you
But I love you even more than that
I still hear you calling me...

Red
Black

Baby Sis.

I remember your heavy hand slapping
Me on the back.
I laughed at you many times
Especially when you whispered!

There's anticipation that what I know
Is not and you'll come back.

To call me Baby Sis
To love the world
To bring sunshine to someone's life.

Rudy,

How I wished you were here,

Because I miss you.

* * *

The feelings stayed with me that day.
Here's another dedicated to my brother:

Feelings

No one knows grief
Until you have experienced it!

The loss of a loved one
Brings many. Many feelings.
GOD HELP ME, HELP US UNDERSTAND

I feel lonely, deserted, alone
I FEEL SAD, MAD
I feel angry, hostile

Why???

Someone I loved DEEPLY
Is gone
Never again can I share
Those moments
I try to …..
But I can't
Not now
GOD PLEASE GIVE ME STRENGTH

I want to run
Away to where?
Away from what?
I just want to run – run – run.

But I sit and remember
And silently say

THANK YOU GOD FOR ALL THOSE YEARS….

Still in my heart of hearts, I talked with
Rudy daily as if he was still right there
listening. I knew he really was listening
and answering me, because I felt him. I
heard him speak to me as only he would or
could. Rudy revealed things I would not
accept. He chastised me when I knew I was
doing something I had no business doing. And
to think he was my younger brother, the one
I tried to hurt earlier in our life.

So here is another tribute to Rudy….
May 18, 1981

Reflections….

Reflections of the past
Thank you God

Because they last.

358 days ago, death struck
your brother is dead
was the news
at 5am on May 25, 1980, a Sunday.

I remember

As if it were just last week,
But instead,

Many days, weeks, months

Have come and gone since that
News first came to me.

The love remains
The memories grow
I remember little things, BIG events
Small gatherings, large functions

My Brother -

Rudy Odis Brown
Was always there.

Like so many others
I've tried to make someone else
Replace my brother.

His uniqueness
His qualities
His love
His ways
His kindness
His faults
His unselfishness
His being
His warmth….
Can never be replaced

Not even imitated…

For there was only one Rudy –
And he's waiting
For us
To join him in his new found
HOMELAND.

At this point in my life I actually stopped
writing about my feelings. Had not
considered I might be depriving the world my
gift. Like Rudy I must share my specialness,
my uniqueness with the world. In essence,
this book is for my brother, who taught me
how to love in such an unlimiting way, it
once scared me to even consider loving so
fully!

The seed from one man, James Armstead,
created me. These are the gardeners who
watered and fertilized me during my growth.

My life has been blessed and enriched by
these men. My Uncles and God-fathers each
have played a significant role in my
development. Each man with his unique
contribution to my unfoldment has aided me
along life's journey. They gave freely of
themselves to me, simply because they loved
me. That is an incredible way to feel and
accept.

Although they are gone, my feelings are deep
for each one of these men that I shared a
special bond with.

William Armstead aka PaPa Hawk

PaPa Hawk, my paternal grandfather. A loner.
Always smiling such a BIG earth brightening
type of broad genuine smile. Whenever we

visited, he was forever walking, never sitting still. He always spoke with kind and gentle words. He was a small man. Seemed like not too much taller than me!

I sense my father received that soft yet lion-like type of strength from PaPa Hawk. He's quiet and uses kind, nurturing words like his father also.

Uncle Buddy received his father's qualities of always visiting neighbors and friends, always walking.

Neither my Dad nor Uncle like to smile. It's too bad because they both have wonderful smiles.

Recently I received a copy of his registered Marriage license and certificate. That was a beautiful gift, dated 30th of May 1914!

<u>Batiste Goff Sr.</u>

My maternal grandfather, Papa T-Boy.

During my childhood somewhere I accepted the fact my grandfather's parents were a slave and slave owner. A lot of us had heard and believed it to be true. Papa T-boy was actually a proud descendant of a German father and Choctaw Indian mother.

The story is they were so deeply in love that when they were told they had to divorce or leave Texas, they left Texas! What a difference in thinking your grandfather was conceived in some primitive, hateful manner as one would envision considering the status of his parents. So many degrading images played in my imagination. The truth of his parents was shared with the family in 1987, just a few years ago. I often think about the family members who never heard the truth, I had considered myself a descendant of violence, rape, human degradation, abuse, etc.. The truth has certainly set me free.

Papa T-boy was very fair skinned. As a matter of fact, most people thought he was a white man. Like the old folks say 'he passed' which means he passed as being accepted as a white man. Papa T-boy worked for the railroad and became a supervisor. That accomplishment would never have been possible for a black man, in Louisiana.

My account of Papa T-boy is mostly derived from others' memory. I did not spend time with him on our vacations to Louisiana because of a challenge my mother had with her father that was not resolved until he was lying on his death bed.

Papa T-boy genes were and are very prominent in his offspring. His great-great-great grandchildren have similarities in their features. I doubt if it will stop there. Perhaps it all began with that strong loving relationship between my Great Grandparents!

Uncle Dave aka Uncle Grass

I loved to see my Uncle dress up. He looked so handsome. What I enjoyed the most was not the smell of bread, he worked and retired from Holsom Bread Co., but the scent of freshly cut grass. My Uncle was forever cutting lawns. As a small child I nicknamed him 'Uncle Grass', a name which stuck until the end. Even when he was confined to bed with Alzheimer's, literally cuffed in restraints he called me 'Grass'. " 'Grass' I need to get out of here. You can do it." He would grab my wrists, pleading for me to help him escape. He was still so strong. I wanted to help, to free him but I couldn't, he was in worse condition than I had known. It hurt me to see my Uncle laying there not remembering from one moment to the next.

Uncle Dave had a special gift of determining the sex of an unborn child. His record was 100% accurate. That was amazing to me. How he did it no one knows for sure, I believe he possessed that gift because of his great love for children, all children.

Uncle Dave and I had a very special relationship, I always followed him around when he was near. It did not matter if we were in Louisiana or California. Everyone knew how much we loved each other.

The sweet, fragrant smell of freshly mowed grass still conjures up a memory of my beloved Uncle. Uncle Grass I love you. You know I would have helped you leave that Nursing home if I could have.
Love you always, Grass

Uncle Joe

One of the elders on my Daddy's side of the family.

Uncle Joe called me 'overcoat' because regardless to the season we traveled I always wore a coat. He would just shake his head in wonder and call me 'overcoat'.

Uncle Joe was the storyteller. I would sit at his feet for hours listening to tales of how my grandfather escaped the terrors of his existence and left slavery. As the next generation began to get old enough to understand, I would gather them up and they would sit with me. We listened contently. The children would not fidget or become restless; we all enjoyed listening to this wise old man. He had a true gift of story telling, you could picture yourself in the scene he was describing.

Thanks Uncle Joe for sharing so freely about our ancestry.

Uncle J.D.

Always smoking a cigar or at least chewing on one.

He drove a school bus for as long as I can remember. Forever wearing a huge smile.

Uncle. J.D. a loving and nurturing soul. I loved to spend time at his home, Uncle J.D. and Aunt Helen made everyone feel completely welcomed. So much warmth in one place, so much love. Always ample food and space. They raised seven wonderful children. Uncle J.D. made sure all of his children went to and graduated from College. Education was very important to him and he instilled that in his offspring.

I can still see him, still smell his cigar, still hear him "'Santa Fee' how's it going gal?" He called me Santa Fee, like the railroad I believe because he could not pronounce my real name La Sandra. Uncle J.D. always had time to talk to me. It did not matter what he was doing, if I told him I needed to talk he stopped and listened. And he had seven children of his own. One would think he got tired of listening to children all day long. In addition he drove that school bus filled with children. When one has a true gift of unconditional love for children then they surround themselves with children constantly. Thanks Uncle J.D. for making me feel like one of your own children! I love you!

Uncle Gerald

Uncle Gerald was the closest in miles, living in Northern California. Most summers I spent at least a part of it with him and his family in San Francisco. Uncle Gerald, Aunt Novella, Novelita and Carmelita were my extra family. I was like the third daughter, I was included and welcomed.

Because of my close relationship with Uncle Gerald I was asked to deliver a message at his funeral. I do not remember what I said either time I spoke. It was an honor to be asked. I did it to express the unconditional love he had always shown me. I cannot describe the bond, like a father never like an uncle.

As I recount each Uncle I remember their smiles. Uncle Gerald had a grand smile. Bright, cheerful, full of mischievous, childlike. You just had to know my Uncle Gerald and you would love him like everyone did, willingly. Words cannot capsulize his personality, he was a marvelous individual.

Uncle Gerald I love you.

Bob Bailey

My God-father, Bob Bailey was a very honest and loving man.

During my childhood I would not see him that often. It was always a good time when I did see him. As a young adult with more courage I asked him one day why he was always 'gone'. He was living with his elderly mother at the time. He respected her and glanced her way to get approval to answer my question. Finally he shared with me about his home away from home. He explained criminal acts and the subsequent punishment when caught. He warned me against unlawful behavior. Encouraged me to keep a level head, do things the right way. Then he told me how he had become a career criminal, how the majority of his life had been spent behind the bars of one jail or another. Locked away from society. He told me all about the types of men who were his other family, fellow inmates. He explained in graphic details the prison environment. I believe his account was so full of details to deter me from any possible acts that would lead to incarceration.

I loved Bob regardless. He told me he didn't know how, anymore, to live on the outside. With a sad, lost soul look in his eyes he told me he loved me! That was the last time I saw my God-father.

Bob, I appreciate your brutal honesty shared with me. I thank you for your unconditional LOVE. I am grateful for the times we had together.

Prentice Westbrook

Puny was my nickname for the father of my closest friend, Carol. We were all short, under 5'4" for sure. I became a second daughter to Prentice and Nellie Westbrook. I was included with gentle care and love. Mr. Westbrook still lived on the same street where we grew up, he never left the neighborhood.

Puny had been sick for a long time. He slipped in and out of remission of cancer. It would hit one part of his body and stop. Then attack another. Puny was a strong Christian, a loving and nurturing spirit, a kind and compassionate man. He never spoke poorly of anyone. Always had a slight smile. Never a frown to be seen on his face.

I arrived in Los Angeles July 2,2001 for a month vacation. Mr. Westbrook was being set up with Home Care, a program for terminally ill patients who desire to die at home. Carol had kept me informed of his health. I desperately wanted to remember his smile, his activity, his kindness. So I kept delaying my visit to the Westbrook's. At one point I even blamed no babysitter for my grandchildren who were traveling with me as an excuse.

I went to see my God-father finally. He had lost so much weight; I could see his bones protruding through his flesh. I sat and talked to him for as long as I could. Talked about my childhood and his influence, thanked him for everything he did so unselfishly for me. Told him jokes and saw a sparkle in his eyes. He was unable to speak, was in the last stages of life.

I remember feeling so blessed to be in Los Angeles during these last moments with him. I could personally thank him for his contributions to my well being. It took me two days before I went to visit. This was highly unusual for me, I always visited my elders on the first day of my arrival to Los Angeles. I took Deja, my granddaughter, with me. Puny had never seen her. But I introduced them and had Deja to kiss him on his cheek. She was so lovable, not being an overactive two year old. She sat with grandma and Mr. Westbrook very quietly.

Two days later I received a call Puny was really in bad shape. I rushed over to be with my other family. That was my first experience of seeing someone minutes from death.

We each took turns visiting with him alone. I said my good bye, thanking him for his awesome presence in my life and kissed him. I knew when I left he would not be alive the next time I saw him. It was such an incredible feeling. Two souls connecting on a higher level. A true spiritual event. As the house filled with relatives, friends, neighbors and Pastors, I departed. I needed to grieve by myself; needed to celebrate his life and homecoming.

PUNY I THANK GOD FOR YOU. I LOVE YOU.
I APPRECIATE YOU. SUCH A WONDERFUL MAN IS
SURELY MISSED BY ALL. WE LOVE YOU.

Fathers

My Daddy - James Armstead

My Daddy- James Armstead, was estranged from my mother and his children while I was very young. Actually too young to remember the details so the earliest times are absent from this writing.

My Daddy is my hero. He has taught me the true meaning of unconditional love. Regardless to what I do, the challenges I face, the lessons in life that I keep relearning, my Daddy is always there with his love. He is the strongest man I know, he's soft spoken and says a lot when he speaks.

Very knowledgeable about life and worldly affairs although he only has a 6th grade education. An extremely spiritual man even though he does not attend a church regularly, he does attend with me when he visits Atlanta. My Daddy is very creative and talented.

Presently we are best friends, sharing thoughts on an almost daily basis. We discuss our strategies about life and love. You see we are both single and working through our reluctance to enter back into the dating arena. My Daddy has always felt my pain, especially recently with the distance between us. Its as if his radar is set on Atlanta! He quietly asks me how I am doing and waits patiently until I tell him the truth. You see I desire to be successful per my definition not his.

My Daddy says I've been successful all my life and he is very proud of me. Still I yearn to have him sit at the head table watching me receive top recognition for my accomplishments. In reality my Daddy has been sitting in that seat for numerous years. He's always championing my causes. There as my biggest and loudest cheerleader. I accept he doesn't always agree with the direction I decide to take, but that just doesn't matter to him. As long as its legal and ethical he supports me. Our relationship has developed over my adult years.

The relationship and communication was difficult during my formative years. My parents were both damaged deeply when their union ended. For both of them many, many years had to pass before the acknowledgement and healing could even begin to occur. I was an adult before reconciliation of broken dreams between them began to emerge.

My father provided financially for me all my life. I remember as a young black girl having my own credit card. My sister and I shopped at name stores in the beach city shopping centers while being a resident of Watts. We shopped in Westchester, a white suburban area of Los Angeles. We were always well dressed.

My Daddy always accepted a quiet role. He was always there, usually right up front - quiet but present. He always shared with me everything he had. Our time together was restricted but he made full use of the time we did have together. He helped supervise our extra curricular activities such as the Woodcraft Rangers. No surprise that he has kept souvenirs from my earliest years. He's very sentimental also. But not the crying kind of emotional person. In fact I've never seen him cry not even when his beautiful wife of 25 years died. I urged him, I begged

him to cry, to release and shed some tears.
If he ever did, it was done in his solitude.
My step-mother, Martha Armstead, shared
openly with me.

We had a very special relationship. I
remember her confiding in me that it was
often difficult for her to accept my Daddy's
unconditional love. Her life with previous
partners were all abusive. For Martha to
have found a generous, sensitive, kind and
loving soul - James Armstead - my Daddy, she
felt truly blessed. She had bouts of not
trusting herself and his love. But she knew,
without a single doubt, that God had
finally heard her cries, her prayers and
Blessed her with a wonderful husband. Martha
- Thank you for loving my Daddy and me!

When I began my career in the modeling
industry my Daddy came to check the company
out. He had his serious, stern face in
place, proudly displayed. I think my Daddy
uses that look as his shield for the world.
Anyway, he visited the facility several
times. He actually interviewed the director.
Of course this was all accomplished
indirectly, very discreetly.

When, however, he gave his stamp of approval
he had grown very fond of the children and
the director. It did not take any time
before he was at the studio everyday. Fixing
up the place, talking with the director,
socializing with the neighbors. He took an
active role, sincere role in developing
UBITQUITDUS into one of Los Angeles'
premiere children modeling companies. The
children, the parents, the staff and the
director all fell in love with my Daddy. He
just loved this new opportunity. The
business escalated into a highly sought

after, professional organization. Our
building had undergone major renovations
led by Mr. Armstead. "Mr. Armstead on behalf
of the entire family of UBITQUITDUS we honor
you as staff person of the year" that was
his crowning glory. He got to walk the
stage just like the models.

During the last years of my career with
Pacific Bell, I traveled a lot. Usually down
to San Diego. My Daddy would come down and
visit because I had been gone for the week.
He'd stay, didn't want any pampering just
wanted to be there for me. My bosses and co
workers alike knew my dad. And still ask
about him to this day. He was my guest of
honor at events honoring my accomplishments.
Yet he supported me when I decided to take
early retirement. He always trusted my
decisions and supports my doing innovated
projects.

One might think I was an only child but I
wasn't. My dad and mom had four and Martha
had two, that was six children total. Daddy
gave and gives of himself to each of us.
Encouraging and supporting us individually
and collectively. Just ask them. And his
many grandchildren are now blessed with his
unconditional love.

I never knew who or how or why I was named.
Had never been asked the question and never
thought to ask it for myself. In 1998, I was
given a class assignment to define my name
and determine why I was named - La Sandra. I
called my Daddy first. Much to my surprise
and amazement I was told a very beautiful
story about how my dad promised to name his
next daughter La Sandra. He was serving in
the US Army during World War II on
assignment in Paris when he

encountered a physically handicapped young girl on the sidewalk. He stopped and chatted with her for a while, he said she was so beautiful. The young girl's mother appeared and lifted her up because she was unable to walk. My dad talked with the mother and she told him her name was La Sandra. My dad was so impressed with her gentle nature, her caring spirit that he wanted to be reminded of that beautiful incident always. I felt a warmth come over me, my name had such a beautiful history and reason.

After leaving the former modeling company I began my own company, Nu Vision Modeling and Entertainment. My dad was more excited and active than I was in creating the best learning institution that the children of South Central Los Angeles were to ever experience. And Thanks to God we accomplished this tremendous feat. We were always actively making improvements, in the community, with the building and most importantly in the lives of the young people. We hosted an International Exchange program with young people from Berlin, Germany. We provided Christmas parties for the neighborhood. We opened our doors to entrepreneurs who just needed a chance. This could not have happened without the support - financially, physically, intellectually, and spiritually- of my Daddy. He was and is always willing to share his wisdom.

At the deepest depths of depression, I sat immobile in the fall of 1992. I know my dad was terrified. His active, vivacious daughter had sentenced herself to the darkness of her house. My Daddy watched over me, prayed with me, read scriptures daily. There was no way he could or would abandon me then. Without his presence I dare not consider what might have been the outcome. I arose, shook the dust off myself and began again, just like he told me to do.

My recovery of life's dilemmas have all been accompanied by my Daddy. The aftermath of two divorces; the death of my younger brother, both step parents and my uncles: the closure of our business and my subsequent relocation. I was moved to relocate to Atlanta after accompanying my son to start at Morehouse College. I actually put off the move until his junior year. At this point I was living with my dad. So to finally have his baby girl share his home then to hear she's moving was a shock to him. It was wonderful living with my dad. My dad refused to accept I was moving until I started bringing boxes home. I was working at an electronics store as a salesperson. It was so funny; my dad had concocted this scheme to keep me in Los Angeles. He went to the store often and developed a friendship with the store manager. Eventually the time came to put his plan into motion. So he had the manager pull me off the sales floor and ask what he could do to make me stay - better hours, switch to another department, what could he do? This was unexpected especially since Dave had already helped with the transfer by giving me a high rated recommendation. When I asked Dave, what was the problem, was he withdrawing his recommendation? He hung his head at that point I felt James - my Daddy's intervention.

Smile I just love him!
Plans continued for the relocation. So my family successfully honored my life by the most loving event - a bon voyage celebration. Of course, my Daddy took a most

active role.

My Daddy is very nurturing without smothering a person. Very strong because of his true soft spirit. Very wise because he shares and does not dictate. Very loving, always loving unconditionally because he loves not because of your actions, he loves just to love.

It took my Daddy years to be able to say 'I love you" to me. I always knew he did, I wanted to hear him say it to me. Just a little thing right? No..wrong! So I said it to him every time we talked, every time we saw each other. The first time he said it, it sounded awkward but it was the most beautiful sound I had ever heard. Now he beats me saying it each time we speak or depart from one another. If this is your challenge, just say it to the person regardless to their response or lack thereof. Watch miracles happen.

THANK YOU DADDY FOR GIVING ME LIFE, OVER AND OVER AGAIN. I LOVE YOU!!!

My Stepfather - Odis Brown

My stepfather was one of the many men of his generation that had been wounded in some way and perhaps never healed before he died of cancer in 1993.

Odis loved my mother. He provided financially for her by showering her with a better way of living, such as new cars, camper, boat, house, fine clothes and jewelry, vacations and the list goes on.

Odis gave of himself to us his step children, he did not use the term, we were always his children. Not sure how, exactly, his financial contributions began or ended because there was no distinction made. As children, we had more, materially, than most of our friends. In fact, Odis always shared openly of his resources-skills, wisdom and talents- with all children. Our friends would often go on fishing and camping trips with us each summer. Providing them with an opportunity to escape the confines of Watts California. We were blessed with those expeditions in the mountains of California. We learned about nature, learned survival skills, learned about life during those camping trips. There was always space for our friends. There was always enough food for our friends.

Although, my mom prepared the meals Odis always made sure there was enough to feed everyone. He was unselfish in his giving. I remember when we had farm animals in our backyard and also on some property near us. We raised chickens, I had a Shetland pony, there were cows and pigs. In Watts that just was not an everyday situation to see. Most people wasn't exposed to that but we were and I am so extremely grateful for those learning experiences. If you have not had the opportunity to raise chickens, pop their neck, boil, pluck the feathers and eat the best fried chicken, you simply do not know what you are missing! Survival skills is what I now call those experiences because we were not forced, by lack of know how, to shop at the grocery store for our food. We had gardens also. Yes Odis was a country man living in the city.

Odis was always building - his life and through construction. He had worked several

different jobs, eventually retiring from Los
Angeles Department of Water and Power (DWP).

I remember, in addition to his full time
position with DWP, he would have side jobs
to do. Forever carrying a 2x4 piece of
lumber and tools. It actually became a joke
with us.

After retirement from DWP, Odis began his
own construction company, Brown and Brown
General Contractors. With little more than a
third grade education he built a very
successful business. By his actions he
demonstrated to us the power of
entrepreneurship. Odis' people skills were
impeccable, he knew how to influence people.
He continued in that same spirit by forming
a family collaborative, Unity-N-Business,
where each family member had to conceive and
develop a unique business idea. The business
was structured, incorporated, developed
completely with all the elements of a
successful endeavor. This business,
I believe, cemented our knowledge and
experiences as business owners. Can you
imagine being a young person and having
lessons like this? It began with us and he
continued to share his wisdom with his
grandchildren and the community at large.
Each of us, the children, have experienced
being an entrepreneur. Most of us can't
abandon the lessons and fulfillment, so even
if someone works for another company, we
mange a personal business as well. Odis'
influence taught us work ethics and
integrity, the how-to's of business
ownership, this includes the grandchildren
as well.

Odis' influence on his grandchildren was and
is awesome. Affectionately known as PaPa, he

always had time to share with them. Educating them; explaining his views of life. Three of his grandsons lived with him during their early formative years. Each of them experiencing a special bonding with PaPa. Its interesting to listen to them describe their individual experiences after many years have passed, its lasting wisdom. Odis had a positive impact on a lot of people, especially the young men. Coaching them, so to speak. Some of our friends did not have fathers in their homes, so Odis was their father. Actually, never making a difference if there was a father figure or not. He taught them as he taught us. And for the many who did have fathers in their homes, he became an extra dad.

Odis was not always available emotionally. We can only show love as we know and understand love. Withdrawal and denial was so common for his generation. Odis consciously gave the best he knew how to give. Odis gave wisdom, gave material things, gave of his time and talent but there was a void in him. It showed in his eyes. He desperately wanted to give fully of himself but something stopped him. I didn't know to ask, how to ask him. But I felt it. Perhaps being open, being vulnerable meant not being a man. Perhaps it meant being soft. The definition of manhood during his coming of age were still marked by only 2 to 3 generations from slavery. Slavery, a time of robbing the soul and spirit of the black man; a time of displacing the family unit; a time of sorrow for the man who cared too deeply. But everyday of his life Odis fought to give his best to his wife, his children, his grandchildren and his neighbors.

My intent is not to say we did not have challenges because indeed we did, and many of them. We must, each of us, choose the way we remember! By choosing the blessings that each person has had on our life, we can readily accept the lessons that came through the process.

The unfulfilled times are omitted. The growing pains are omitted. The unmet expectations are omitted. Not because of choosing denial, rather choosing acceptance of things that were, things that can only be changed by my attitude and perception. Odis demonstrated love the best way he knew how. And it did not always look the way the children might have wanted it to look. So what if it didn't match the TV version of fantasyland? I value all the lessons Odis taught me about life.

Pops - Elihu Rodgers

My father (in-law) forever. That was our promise to one another a few years back!

Pops calls me 'Little Sandy' as his term of endearment. I accept my father-in-law loves me unconditionally, both me and my son. He has always accepted me just the way I am, even while going through challenges with his son. Just always available for me, Simply Pure Love.

Whenever I visit my in-laws, Pops and I always manage to share private talks together. We talk about my life, my son, sports - especially those Lakers! , current events and while they were living his parents. Our bond is unbreakable. Even Mom, Mrs. Rodgers, who is inclined to not allow any female too close, received me with open arms from the very beginning and allowed me time alone with her husband. One just has to know Mom to truly understand that statement. It was an honor to me once I understood just how incredibly jealous she was of all females. Mom never ever allowed any woman time alone with her Rodgers! They both knew my love was and remains sincere in every way humanly possible. And even though I am no longer married to his baby boy, Pops still proclaims Little Sandy will always be his daughter. He has even told me that whoever I date and/or marry will become a son to him. Now that's hilarious!

I think to myself, how will my ex handle his ex's husband as his brother!! You must admit that conjures up an incredible vision.

After my first divorce, more about that in a later chapter, I lost all contact with Mom and Pops. When Kevin and I reconciled our differences and decided to get back together Pops was elated. He made me promise not to ever lose contact again and I have kept my word even with the final divorce from his son.

Pops' parents lived in Los Angeles in a house he had purchased for them many years before when he convinced them to relocate. Pops has and continues to be a very generous man. He had a wife and five children but he saved his money to purchase his parents a home in the city where he lived. Pops was not a wealthy man. He did however have his priorities in the proper order. His parents' welfare was extremely important to him and he simply did what he knew he had to do. Pops is also a very humble individual. His parents were well taken care of by him. I would visit Granddad and Grandmother as often as I could. They were such special people. I understood where Pops got his admirable qualities. Granddad died in June of 1992. Pops had reserved a seat for me in the family car. But I couldn't attend the funeral. Pops was hurt badly by my absence. I had to confess the truth to him, why I wasn't there when he needed me. Kevin and I were experiencing a terrible time. Not only was divorce the solution, a restraining order was in place. I had filed for the order therefore Kevin was not allowed within one thousand feet of me. 'I' had filed the order, I was engulfed in pain. Granddad was Kevin's grandfather and I felt I didn't belong. If I hadn't filed the restraining order I would have gone. Kevin and I were fighting so badly that he missed the funeral also. My sister was the first person to tell him that his grandfather had died. That was such a pain filled time. It had only been eight months since my hysterectomy, which was October 1991. Kevin and I were having challenges then but they were subtle, or so I thought.

The recovery period following a hysterectomy is six weeks. My Pops visited me every single day. He made sure I had eaten my meals, taken my medication and getting my rest. He was there to take care of me. That was very important, a particular type of bonding that's difficult to explain. Here it was me barely getting along with his son and I'm sure he knew it. By my bedside everyday to nurse me back to total health. Pops is my Angelic Hero.

Grandmother, Pops' mother, was very petite 4'10" or shorter. Grandmother became more sickly after her husband passed. I spent more and more time with her. Whenever she went into the hospital I was there. Even when her vision was so damaged she could hardly recognize anyone by sight, she always knew when I visited. Each time she would say "You know I can't see, who are you?" My answer every time was the same, 'Well if you don't know who I am I had better go home.' Grandmother would break into laughter and say "Oh that's my Little Sandy". She and I had a very warm and loving relationship. Perhaps she knew but its possible she didn't. I love my elders. I love listening to their wisdom. With Grandmother it was no different, I would sit and listen to her for hours. And yes sometimes she rambled. It was an honor to be with her. My birth grandparents had all been deceased since the early 70's. For Pops, my time with his mother meant more to him than he's ever been able to verbally explain. An experience that penetrated his heart with gratitude. Grandmother made her transition in January 1997.

Pops has spent most of his life providing for and taking care of other people, his parents, wife and children, siblings, grandchildren and the host of friends he has made over the years. So when he suffered a stroke in January 2001, we were all in shock. Pops is a strong, masculine person who is physically fit, routinely participating in some form of exercise. He has found joy in helping others. But now that's all changed. The same ones he has helped throughout the years are in a position to give back to this wonderful man. For Pops, receiving help was difficult to adjust to. He is still recovering. He is adamant about doing his physical therapy yet still uneasy about allowing others to help him. From our conversations I know this has been extremely difficult for him. He's always been the source of strength, and now he needs help.

To know my Pops is to understand he does not always finish a thought or sentence. Frequently he mispronounces words. One thing is absolute, his unconditional love for those he cares about. Pops is warm, loving, compassionate, wise, humble, honest, trustworthy, all the superlatives that can be used to describe a true MAN.

Pops I Love You Now and Forever. I will always be your "Little Sandy".

Uncle Buddy - aka The Wolf

Uncle Buddy is my eldest living relative. Actually my only Uncle that is still living. The Wolf, as a lot of friends call him, is very dear to me, he is eighty seven years young!

He has lived in California all of my life. Everyone has a special story of their own to tell how he has impacted their lives. He is very special to a lot of people, relatives and neighbors alike. The Wolf plainly described, just loves people. He will gladly give his last of anything to anyone who is in need. He is extremely free hearted, generous in spirit, very independent, nurturing and wise. Uncle Buddy is a widow, his loving wife Aunt Thelma died many years ago.

Our relationship deepened, became stronger after my retirement. This was due to the fact I had more time to spend with him. We did many things together. By this time his eyesight had worsened and he was unable to drive a vehicle. So I became his driver, chauffeur, almost like 'Driving Miss Daisy!' Instead it was Driving The Wolf. We had fun together. Uncle Buddy's demeanor with most people is 'friendly' disagreements. He is forever in opposition with folks. But not with me, we always talk from our hearts with each other. Our relationship, our bond caused the little ugly jealousy monster to come alive within several souls in our family, Uncle Buddy's and my immediate family. We just did not care.

Before my retirement and while his vision was still good Uncle Buddy had a very lucrative lawn care service business. He was an excellent business man, largely due to his trustworthiness. He had keys to the homes of most of his clients. That always seemed unusual, but people trusted him.

Uncle Buddy has lived in the same house for more than thirty years. All the neighbors up and down the street, young and old, established residents and newly relocated alike all know him. He has served on the executive board of the Block Club for many years as the Treasurer. He takes his responsibility very serious and is good at his job. Uncle Buddy walks the neighborhood daily, helps his closest neighbors with anything he can do for them - he is the rock on the block!

When my son went away to College I rented out my house. It had gotten too big for just me. Uncle Buddy graciously opened up his home to me. I lived with him and his youngest son, Kenny, for almost a year. This was the beginning of our camaraderie. We would go to lunch at the Sizzler Restaurant, that was his favorite place to eat. We became regular customers, the staff all knew us and expected us. They even allowed me to purchase my meals at senior citizen prices! We would sit and joke for hours.

In 1994, Uncle Buddy started having some health challenges. I would take him to the doctor, I was his emergency contact person. One day I received a call saying I had to rush him to emergency as soon as possible. Within an hour we were at the hospital. He had prostrate problems, had been bleeding and the situation was critical. His blood count was dangerously low. I had no idea it was quite that bad.

I did know he had fainted several times and that was what prompted me to get him to the doctor in the first place. I stayed with him the entire time; spoke with the doctors and nurses. I sat there during his surgery, walked along side the gurney as they wheeled him to the operating room. The hospital staff assumed I was his daughter! And that created problems for my cousin, Wanda, Uncle Buddy's youngest daughter. I was willing to step aside because Uncle Buddy didn't deserve to have conflict going on while he was recovering from his surgery.

But when the doctor told him what had happened, that his daughter did not want me to know about his condition, Uncle Buddy had me to come into his room as he explained to the doctor that I was to be told everything! I took care of Uncle Buddy when he was released. Wanda and I worked out our differences. I told her I was not attempting to replace her role, I had the time whereas she was working and had three children to care for.

All was Well. Others in my immediate family became resentful as well, we had dealt with these same issues before so Uncle Buddy and I were prepared.

Uncle Buddy has always defended me and my actions. He will not allow anyone, not even my mother or my father, his brother to say anything negative about me. At times that caused strife for him, he just didn't care. He felt he was my protector and he served in that capacity faithfully and still does. No one goes to him any longer with negative remarks concerning me.

Uncle Buddy stays in contact with my friends that he knows personally. I can always count on one of them to tell me they had recently talked with him. Now whenever I visit California I spend as much time as possible with Uncle Buddy. Help him with anything that needs to be done, going to doctor appointments, paying his bills, running errands, it doesn't matter. As he often asks me "Got any running space?", I know that means he needs help. He's a very proud man and doesn't like to ask for help. He feels people know his vision is poor and he can't drive. He feels he should not have to ask, they should offer and I agree with him.

Uncle Buddy has always been honest with me. Forever supportive of choices I have made. I thank God for his undying love. I have learned how to resolve delicate family issues with him. I have learned survival skills from him, how to continue when the world seems against your every move.

Uncle Buddy, Wolf…I Love You!!

My Brothers

George Tofforo

I feel my oldest brothers' pain as I write about our relationship, his life and the distance that now separates us.

I had very proudly accepted the 'peace maker' role in my family, especially between my siblings. Constantly the go-between when disputes occurred. Always the light in the darkness of ego fighting. My sister and brothers all love each other tremendously. Like most normal families there were times of disagreements. Each one of us is so strong willed in our own individual beliefs that resolving challenges was not always easy. Our egos so huge nothing could penetrate them even when we knew we were not behaving in a loving manner. So when I decided to leave home and relocate to Georgia it was difficult for my family to accept.

They were all extremely supportive of my decision especially since it meant I would be close to my only child. They each loved my courageousness to start a new life in a new state. But the miles weren't the only distance between us. They felt, as I have recently been told, I deserted them. The emotional distance has grown to be greater than the physical distance, particularly between George and I.

I have, without fail, looked up with respect to my oldest brother. He always appeared larger than life to me. I have always been the runt of the family, the smallest one. There is seven years difference between us. George was always so mature, so grown. He was my idol. As children, I remember George was always running away from home. I don't know how many times it was actually, but it seemed like all the time. He would forget to take something he needed with him, sneak back and ask me, his baby sister to get it for him while he hid outside. I felt so honored that he trusted me to get his things, more importantly that he trusted me not to tell our parents. I wore the badge of George's confidant. To a young girl those secrets were bigger than life itself. I often wondered why he ran away so much. All I knew was I was so happy when he returned.

George is a very caring and loving spirit, gives freely of his resources and genuinely loves life. We shared so much together. We were always available for each other, to help each other through the tough times.

George has fully supported and encouraged me with each of my business endeavors. George gave willingly and willfully of his time, talent and money to restoring my modeling facility in Los Angeles when it was severely damaged during the Rodney King riots. He never complained, he just did the necessary work. And when the business was in need of structure and expansion George brought in an excellent friend of his to assist with the company's growth. Actually, George brought in several people to aide in Nu Vision's growth. Once again, his presence, his acknowledgement of my efforts meant everything to me.

Perhaps my leaving Los Angeles was a reminder of his childhood, feelings of abandonment. I miss my big brother tremendously. George I love you very deeply. I have not deserted you. I only live in a different place. The huge space in my heart is and always will be reserved just for you.

I know that sometimes the activities of living keeps us so occupied that little room is left. Please accept my apologies if I opened up old wounds for you. I am still your little sister and I LOVE YOU AND MISS YOUR PRESENCE IN MY LIFE!

George I thank you so much for loving me, just the way I am. For teaching me about life. I thank you for your contributions towards my well being. I thank you for being unselfish. I thank you for the blessings and lessons that we shared.

George is married to a very beautiful woman, Brenda. Brenda loves George unconditionally, it shows in her eyes and by the way she looks at him. Thanks Brenda for loving my big brother.

George, you know that peace you have been searching for? Longing for? That inner peace that surpasses all understanding, tranquility? Well Big Brother I've found it. It's definitely on the inside of each of us. You cannot find it anywhere in the outer world. I watched your long stretches of solitude, your journeys to the mountains and beaches, your relentless quest to be at peace within yourself. It's there, trust me. Not in the library of books you've read or seminars you've attended. It's in your heart, in your soul.

My Gift To You - be still and know, God and Love is all there is.

William Saafir

William is like my oldest twin, the one that was delivered first. For most of our lives endeavors, same missions, side by side like twins.

William is two years older. He preceded me in school. My brother is intellectually brilliant, very astute. He mastered learning early in life and continues to amaze me with his wealth of knowledge. He was a Rhodes Scholar finalist! I secretly resented him growing up. Not because of his ability rather the teachers always expected me to perform like him or better. Sometimes I just wanted to goof off. The first day of school each semester in each class was the same.
I would be questioned, "You're William Armstead's sister aren't you? I expect great things from you!"

Don't misunderstand I enjoyed learning and school also, perhaps just not as much as William. I followed in his footsteps, playing with the orchestra, being very active in the student government programs and so on. There was just no down time and my spirit needed that.

I think being a tomboy as a young person was heavily influenced by being able to hang around William and his friends. I was hanging around them and they didn't seem to care. I loved playing sports, especially baseball.

In the early 60's, William and I became relentless in the challenge of changing our community of Watts. A community, a ghetto plagued by despair and hopelessness. We could not accept the negative stigmatism and decided to take a very active role in the transformation of our community. SCFIW, Student Committee For the Improvement In Watts was born. We were blessed to have an

unselfish and very caring teacher/mentor-
Ms. Sue Welsh to guide and lead us towards
our goals. The experience was exhilarating
for a group of young people who had been
wearing the shackles of discouragement.

We were willful teenagers bucking the
system. We demanded attention and respect.
We settled for nothing less than complete
cooperation from everyone - other teenagers,
adults, teachers, community leaders and
finally our elected political officials.
Can you picture a group of teenagers from
any major degraded community,
marching/rallying and insisting on immediate
improvement in their neighborhood? If it's
difficult for you to picture this, you are
not alone. The politicians went as far as to
laugh at our initial visit.

Persistence and dedication to achieving our
goals concluded our biggest project of
repairing the elder residents homes, having
abandoned and dilapidated buildings
renovated or destroyed and a joint Community
Pride Celebration, 'Dancing In The Streets',
a popular song at that time. The Watts Riots
erupted shortly after that victory and our
efforts were short lived. SCFIW made a
positive impact on the attitudes of folks
living in Watts, the politicians that served
our community and gave us as the members, a
great sense of pride and accomplishment.

William graduated with honors and a full
scholarship to Wilberforce University. He
left Watts to attend college in Ohio. This
was during the awesome era of The 'Black
Power Movement' that was exploding across
the United States.

William subsequently became a member of the
Nation Of Islam, a very strong FOI – Fruit
of Islam-student. As with every other
endeavor, he has become a scholar of the
teachings and is currently an Imam,
religious leader/elder. Although he prefers
a lesser role in the Muslim Community, he
cannot forsake his inherent ability to be a
leader.

Our family, including me, did not fully
understand what the fundamental issues were
with the Muslims. We allowed ourselves to be
educated by the mass media as to how we
should re-act to William. Criticism was
common place. Fear took a stronghold on all
of us. William was rejected because of his
beliefs. I must admit, the movement was
extremely radical, according to what we had
been taught all of our lives about religion.

Against everything that Negroes had accepted
about themselves as truths. Plus Muslims did
not eat pork! Not even eat food that was
cooked in a pot that had ever contained
pork. I trusted my brother; I needed to
learn more about his new found religion. I
was the only family member, in his early
association, that allowed myself the freedom
to seek understanding of the Nation Of
Islam.

Their doctrine was awesome, liberating and
the leader Honorable Elijah Mohammad was a
dynamic speaker. I read the books, I asked
questions and I liked this new knowledge.
Although I have not become a Muslim, I
totally respect my brother and all Muslims.
Their teachings are based on the Koran and
Universal Truths. You simply cannot argue
with TRUTH! I have become friends with many
Muslims

nationwide and have attended every gathering possible, have worshiped at the Mosque from Los Angeles to Atlanta and in between.

As-Salaam-Alaikum,

I love you my Muslim Brothers and Sisters!

William, married to a very beautiful woman Stephanie, had two gorgeous daughters – Arletta and Latifah, returned to Los Angeles. William's family was subjected to ridicule by family and friends. Lack of knowledge and/or understanding will cause people to act in fear-filled ways.

William has never ever backed down or denied what he believes in. This wholehearted attitude was demonstrated repeatedly with regards to his beliefs in the Nation of Islam. He did not waiver. He attempted to educate but few honestly listened. As William and Stephanie's family grew, so did the criticism. They have seven beautiful children, all who have graduated from high school have scored in the top 10 percentile on SAT scores, nationally.

Stephanie home schooled them through the majority of their learning. They are fluent in the Arabic language. The eldest children have attended and graduated from college. Our family thought his children would be somehow damaged by their lack of material possessions. Looking closely at the true meaningful ingredients of life and family, one would know without doubt they have and had everything they needed. Unconditional Love!

William, without consciously being aware of it, proved to the rest of us that materialism had little effect in a nurturing family environment.

William left California again and perhaps for the last time in 1986, incidentally twenty years after his first departure. This time his mission was the establishment of a self-sustaining community in Weatherford Texas. The majority of the residents were Muslim but it was not a restricted community.

There was probably a mixture of feelings for both his wife and children concerning the move. All has proved well in that decision.

The bond between William and I have become stronger in our years of maturity. We still envision a better environment in which to live. We are each TRUTH students in our respective religions. We earnestly seek empowerment and freedom of thought for ourselves and the community.

William has grown through various business ventures. His true nature is a leader and a teacher. He is so confident and compassionate. He is strong in being a servant to humankind. He is a scholar and community organizer. He is a strong human rights activist.

I pray for my brother's strength through the challenges he is currently facing and will face as he crusades against inhumane treatment of any human. William, I Love You so much. I thank God for you and I thank you for allowing God to express through you in such a powerful manner. May you live long enough on this earthly plane to witness 'New Africa' fully and completely functioning as a thriving International Business force. Thanks for always sharing your wisdom and insights with me. Thank you for constantly being a Loving person through all of life's circumstances and challenges. Thanks for loving me, unconditionally, without limits, restraints or conditions.

BoBo - Marvin Charles Baker

Throughout my life, from childhood, my best of friends have remained male. I choose the word male to cover all age groups of men. I was a tomboy growing up. I would rather be playing softball, football (tag), fishing or any number of activities that were considered 'for boys'. I was always hanging out or hanging around my brothers and their friends. I believe the friends accepted me because I played pretty good ball!

My closest friend, my play brother, growing up was BoBo. His parents named him Marvin Charles Baker but back in our younger days we were all given a nickname. BoBo resulted from an inability of one of his siblings to pronounce brother. Strange how names are created and stay with us, all of our lives.

BoBo and I were literally inseparable. If you saw one of us, you knew the other was not too far behind. BoBo's mother died at an early age and BoBo stayed with us most of the time after her death. BoBo associates 'The Christmas Song' with his mother; he could not remain dry eyed for long whenever he would hear it on the radio.

We remained the best of friends throughout the years. We got in trouble together. We defended each other whenever necessary. We loved each other without question. He was and is my brother for all intent and purposes. I have not seen BoBo in about eight years.

Through his marriages, my marriages, our children, we remained. I miss him, enormously, sharing with him. Want to express my love to him. Although I know BoBo knows I love him I would like to express my appreciation to him. He helped me with and through a lot of challenging times. He didn't judge me, spoke from the place in his heart that accepted me unconditionally. He loved me unconditionally; would be offended if boyfriends or husband mistreated me, made me unhappy. BoBo always told me the truth, especially when I appeared not to want to listen. It was those times I was in the deepest of denial and he knew it. He would not allow me to wallow, drown myself in self pity.

We learned how to dance at the same time, again together. We especially loved to do the Cha Cha. We entered dance contests as a couple, we were always practicing our steps. We just performed so well together, synchronized dancing is what its called today. We were simply the best dancing couple around town! We knew each other so well, we were always in harmony with one another. Pure excellence on the dance floor!

Only those men who were attempting to say hurtful words to me ever uttered an unkind description of the relationship I shared with BoBo. I made sure people, especially the men in my life, understood my relationship with BoBo was non-negotiable. BoBo did the same with the people in his life. Everyone accepted our relationship. Actually there was nothing anyone could do to destroy it. We had a special bond, as close as blood, if not closer. We were closer than blood because we chose each other and we did not happen to just be born into the same family! I vaguely remember piercing our fingertips and becoming blood relatives. At some point in time when a friendship was destined to go the full extent, to express its sincerity, people performed the blood connection. Both parties pierces their finger and blood is swapped - thus blood brother or sister. That was safe in our young lives!

BoBo and I went to the same elementary, junior and senior high schools together. He is one year older, so we spent at least two years on the same campus of both junior and senior high school. We were shadows of each other. Let me share a funny story with you. One day while we were attending Davis Starr Jordan High School in Watts, BoBo came up to me. He was twitching and acting very silly. I laughed because I thought he was playing a trick on me, which he did most of the times. I told him to stop. I went to walk away, told him I couldn't be late for my next class. I remember it so clearly. As I turned back to BoBo he was falling on the ground. He was having an epilepsy seizure and needed to find me to tell because he knew I would take care of him. Panic came but I refused to allow it to take control.

Forgot about class and being late - I had to take care of my brother. So even as kids we knew if no one else existed to protect us, we did that for each other.

In essence, BoBo was the first male outside
of my immediate family of brothers, cousins
and uncles that I learned to love
unconditionally. We experienced so much of
life together. Learned how to handle
challenges together, did not permit other
people to destroy our bond, we deeply loved
each other.

BoBo, I Love You so much. Thank you for
supporting me when no one else believed in
me and my goodness. Thank you BoBo for
sharing without thought of return. BoBo, you
are so very, very dear to me. If you are
reading this book, by some chance, Please
Call or write to me. Love always through the
ages and beyond.

David Steven Brown

My baby brother. I actually watched his
birth into this world, January 3, 1961. I
was 10 and Mom Brown, our next door neighbor
was watching me as my mother was giving
birth. I managed to sneak away, climbed up
on the fence and peered through the window
as my brother was being delivered. It was
definitely an experience I will always
remember.

I left home at age eighteen; Stevie was just
seven. Most of his formative years I was not
present in the home. Either away at college
or experiencing my own young adulthood. I do
recall that as a teenager a lot of my
weekend time was spent babysitting my two
younger brothers. Of course I resented the
fact that my friends had less responsibility
than I did. While they were able to do
things I was confined to babysitting. That
is just a typical teenager response to not

having complete autonomy. Anyway I left at eighteen, returned ten years later for about six months after my breakup with Jeff.

In my family as in many families, when there is a gap between siblings, the younger ones are often spared certain restrictions and rules. So it was with my youngest brother, Stevie. I guess Mama and Odis were exhausted from the experiences in raising the older children. But with that tiredness came a lack of rules to govern ones self by. Stevie was freer to do certain things that the older children were not allowed to do. Instead of helping I feel it caused a great deal of insecurity for Stevie and a distance from his older siblings. Stevie constantly feels the need to prove himself to others, that he has all the answers and does not need advice.

During his lifetime he has erected a huge brick wall around his heart concerning his siblings. Perhaps we older siblings failed him; the oldest left to join the military when he was just a baby; Janice left home when he was three; William left the state when Stevie was five and I left when he was seven. There was definitely physical distance, every two years another one was leaving!

Stevie was spoiled with too much freedom and materialism. He has gauged a person's worth by what they possessed. As he matures in life, my prayer is that he will come to accept a person's worth cannot and must not be measured by the size of their bank account or house but by the content of their character and heart.

Stevie learned early in his life not to depend on his older siblings to be there for him, because we weren't. I am certain a void remains due to our absence.

As Stevie experienced challenges in his first marriage he would call and talk with me. I remember very vividly one such call. Stevie was calling from Martin Luther King Hospital and wanted me to pick him up. He had been shot!

Stevie recounted the story to me, he and his wife were having an awful fight. He left and returned with their youngest son. As he lifted up his son, his wife shot him through the iron security door. This was indeed the most important conversation I was to have ever had with my baby brother. I was careful not to place blame or accuse either of them of being wrong. I prayed for strength and wisdom to share with him what would be most valuable. I told him I loved him. I told him there needed to be distance put between him and his wife for awhile, to work through their problems. My main concern was the safety and well being of my brother.

My intentions were misunderstood, I was accused of attempting to break up their marriage simply because I was divorced! I was devastated, had been rejected by my family for something I didn't even say. I remained detached from my family emotionally. I watched as my youngest brother suffered through one loss after another. Until everything was gone, his home, cars, boats, family, pride, family owned business. He had reached the bottom and had difficulty reaching out and asking for help.

I love my brother very much. I am proud of his accomplishments in life. He has five wonderful children whom he adores. Stevie has a wonderful wife, Ada. Ada and Stevie got a second chance at happiness. They dated during high school, got married to other people, later to be joined together again. They are blessed to have found the other again, in love.

I still feel I need to impart some wisdom to my brother. Our egos can be so strong, we can deny the sharing, either by becoming frustrated at explaining what I need to say or by refusing to listen because he has it all figured out. After all I wasn't around when he needed me most.

My dearest Stevie, You are a beautiful, intelligent human being. I apologize if I was not present to help you through your younger years. I love you very much. Life is a journey. One does not get to a destination and say that's the end. We must experience fully with love each step of the journey. Learn to relax and enjoy the essence in life and nature. Stop to listen to the birds' melody and see the rich bright colors of the flowers. You are whole and complete within yourself. Trust and accept you are never alone. God is always with you, guiding and protecting you along the way.

You need not, must not attempt to control the outcome of everything. Remember each of us, especially our children have their own specific journey in life they must experience by themselves to learn their lessons in life. Release and let go, trust God to work it out through you.

P.S. Don't tell God how it must look!!
(Smile)
Know that I love you unconditionally...
Now and forever.

Glenn Harold Armstead

My cousin, my brother, spiritual student and teacher, my confidant and my friend. We share agape love!

Glenn and I became very close during our twenties. Cannot pinpoint the exact year but I believe it was after his younger brother, Bruce, died that we really began our bonding. We had shared times together during our childhood as our families would vacation. Glenn was born, raised and still lives in Houston Texas.

Glenn is currently married to a very beautiful and extremely spirited woman, Ida. Ida is a strong Christian woman, she loves Glenn unconditionally. Glenn has two children, a son and daughter. Glenn is extremely active in his church, serving as a Deacon and Treasurer. Those are merely titles, his devotion to his spiritual life and upliftment of the family and community far surpasses any descriptive title bestowed upon him. Mainly because he has made a very conscious and concerted decision to be a dedicated servant. To serve humanity to his best ability.

Back in our twenties however life was very, very different. We each found ourselves ultimately in unhealthy relationships. We both possibly stayed longer than we needed to. We hurt so badly but ending our marriages was extremely difficult. Each beating ourselves up so badly it did not allow for anyone to demean us. Glenn and I exercised a special kind of love for one another. In the end Glenn stayed longer in his first marriage than I did. We were in unhealthy relationships not because we married bad people but because we were unhealthy in our own souls. Glenn and I did not know whose - God - we were. We had not defined ourselves nor truly loved ourselves. We were looking outwardly for the love that only we could give ourselves. We didn't understand that then. Our search included jobs, alcohol, spouses and children. Desperately looking for love in all the wrong places. I am positive that our spouses hurt just as much as we did, if not more. Praise God for renewal.

Glenn experienced a huge void in his life and heart following the deaths of his father, mother, grandmother and his younger brother, Bruce.

From our conversations I felt Glenn had difficulty sharing his pain with others, especially his immediate family. Perhaps it was because Glenn felt his siblings hurt and was grieving the deaths as well. We talked about the inevitable void in his life for years.

My younger brother, Rudy, had been tragically killed in an automobile accident just like Bruce. They were both in their early twenties. We shared our losses with compassion and love. Secretly in our own hearts we wished God would have spared our younger brothers' lives by taking ours. Glenn and I had many similarities.

When my son, Malcolm, was born Glenn protected him like a Mother Hen. Whenever Glenn was around no one else could hold or care for Malcolm. Glenn was truly a Godfather to my son. He just naturally accepted that role. He has always cared for Malcolm, always protecting and guiding him.

In 1994 as Malcolm was driving by himself from Atlanta to attend a Family Reunion in Louisiana, he became the target of racist police harassment. When I received the news that my son had been arrested I was horrified. What do I do? When Glenn heard the news he just took control. He assured me everything would be okay. As we made the drive to the jail, Glenn kept a watchful eye on me. Glenn handled all the details once we arrived at the jail. Surely another member of my family could have helped but Glenn did not allow them. Malcolm was his boy and he would handle it. Thanks Glenn for loving my son so very much.

Glenn is an exceptional father to his own son, Stephfan. Stephfan has been going through a rather rebellious stage for a few years. This ate away at Glenn's heart. He would often ask what he had done wrong as a father and what could he do to help his son. Glenn had done everything humanly possible to shield his son from the path in life he was now deciding to travel.

Eventually, after many conversations, Glenn accepted Stephfan had his own journey in life to make. Glenn loves his son unconditionally, keeps him in his daily prayers and appropriately insists on respect from him. Stephfan is deeply loved by his family. Glenn particularly anticipates his return home, like the Prodigal son.

Glenn learned to bury his problems in a liquor bottle. He drank heavily and often. At the time it became his only means of survival through the pains he was feeling, engulfed with, had become prey to, Glenn faced the demon head on and decided he could and would destroy it! Glenn has been clean and sober for the last seven years. Thanks God for healing.

Glenn pays tribute to me for helping him through the messes of his life. I am here today healthy and sane because of my relationship with Glenn. He has rescued me literally, from numerous events in my life. In early 1994 I left California driving round trip to Louisiana helping someone handle some personal business. As fate would have it I got stranded! I had no way home. Glenn came to my rescue, coming to get me from Louisiana and buying my airplane ticket back to Los Angeles. I was devastated by the experience, felt betrayed by the person I had unselfishly helped to make that long drive. Conversations with Glenn eased my tensions and bitterness. Thanks Glenn for always sticking with me.

And when my granddaughter, Deja, had been rushed to emergency suffering from an acute asthma attack, I called Glenn. Glenn joined me in prayer concerning her health. I am happy to announce that was Déjà's last time being rushed to the hospital although she had suffered with severe asthma attacks for more than a year!

Glenn possesses excellent oratorical skills, as some may call it a 'gift to gab'. But I listen and hear the profound wisdom in what he has to share. Glenn remains my confidant to this very day, especially with matters of the heart. I am always open and honest with my feelings with him. I feel drawn to dig deeper inside my heart to share.

Glenn, I so thank God for you! Your love, your presence, has carried me through so much in my short lifetime! I Love You – Glenn Harold Armstead!!

Sons

The biggest influence I had on the lives of the men I closely associated with in Los Angeles resulted in their fulfillment of professional dreams. From pursuing dreams of becoming an artist, engineer, TV personality, opening a beauty salon, expanding existing business to helping to build the largest minority owned modeling company in southern California. This was all done without fore thought, all done with love, admiration and support of the individuals' dream.

In Atlanta, each young man that I have spent endless hours with as a surrogate mother has all fulfilled their personal dreams. Each one is now married and as one gets engaged or seriously involved another pops into my life.

Now I tell each young man that even though they may not currently have a romantic partner that in its proper time they will depart from me to join in holy matrimony. That statement has not always been received with an open heart because each man began his relationship with me single and unattached. I don't say it at the beginning of the friendship.

As the friendship deepens I can sense they are being prepared for a holy union. It has proven true with each man. I do not match make. For the most part I don't even know the woman they ultimately choose. I can't explain the movement, it has just repeated itself each time. God has used me to help these young men along their journey in life.

I am happy and excited about the contributions I have made to each of these

young men in Los Angeles and Atlanta. I will
continue to allow God to use me in whatever
capacity is appropriate for all involved.

God always has a divine plan for our lives.
I wanted a house full of children. God gave
me one and an ever growing number of
children across the United States. Thanks
God.

Darryl Hood

April 22, 1997

Dear Sandy,

*As you know I am currently one of the
Weekend Anchor/ Reporters at KQTV in St.
Joseph, Missouri. I wanted to take the time
to let you know that you are in part
responsible for my success in the career
that I have chosen. During my time at Nu
Vision, your guidance and advice taught me
that I could be successful at whatever I
chose to do with my life.*

*Nu Vision also provided me with the
confidence I needed to take the first step
to realizing my dreams. With every goal that
I accomplish, my confidence grows stronger.
Sandy, thank you for everything that you and
Nu Vision have done for me. The time that I
spent with the company had a very positive
impact on my life. Keep up the good
work!*

Love your protégé,
Darryl Hood

I have known Darryl all of his life. His
grandmother, Maxine, and my stepmother,

Martha, had been neighbors and were the best of friends.

Each year my Daddy and Martha hosted a Christmas party. Complete with a Santa Claus, gifts for each child and an elaborate meal. Darryl's family was always present. 'Cool" as he was called as a young child was the eldest in the family. Darryl has always been a serious individual, an observer of life, studying intently.

When Darryl began his modeling career at Ubitquitdus we became closer. Darryl studied and perfected his modeling techniques, remaining the serious student. At this time Malcolm and Darryl were young teenagers. He started to join us more in our outings. Malcolm and Darryl formed a bond, a friendship and several business ventures. They were two hard working business men (teenagers).

When I opened Nu Vision Modeling Darryl was one of the staff members and models. Darryl studied and learned the business aspects of the company. Always an excellent runway model, he was also a role model to all who visited our facility. Darryl was an asset and contributed heavily to the company's huge success. He solicited and booked shows, he trained the models, he did whatever was necessary and did it exceedingly well. Others often called Darryl my protégé.

People knew I maintained high standards for myself and Nu Vision, indeed which was an honor for Darryl. He could handle all aspects of the company's performance anywhere we appeared. Darryl could instruct the models, knew the routines, model himself and commentate the shows. At this point in his life Darryl preferred to be called Suave. We all respected his wishes. Consistently he was professional, determined, sincere, dedicated and trustworthy.

Darryl decided he wanted to become a TV personality. He would watch the news intently, studying their gestures, facial expressions and voice inflections. With support of the staff Darryl began writing the prominent Ms. Pat Harvey. Persistence paid off for Darryl. He wrote letters and received no reply. He called the station, he never quit.

And as a result Ms. Harvey agreed to mentor him. Darryl graduated from Cal State Northridge University and has been on a steady climb up the ladder of life. I re-learned persistence from Darryl. Darryl has worked in various news positions throughout the United States.

Currently Darryl is News Anchor for FOX5 in Las Vegas, Nevada and has been featured as one of the most eligible bachelors in Nevada.

Darryl took his first airplane trip with me and Malcolm as he left to attend college in Atlanta. Darryl enjoyed the adventure. This was shortly after completing the Model Expo '92.

When I relocated to Atlanta in 1995, Darryl made the long drive with me. That was his first cross-country experience. We listened to self-empowering tapes, talked about our goals and dreams; had a wonderfully exciting adventure.

Darryl is an aspiring student of life. A role model for his younger siblings who have each attended college and travels Internationally. Darryl himself loves exploring the world.

I am so extremely proud of Darryl's accomplishments. He started out in very humble surroundings of Watts California. He refused to allow where he grew up to determine or limit his success.

Lesson: When adults give the best they have to children, it offers them more opportunities. My challenge to each person reading this book is to commit to mentoring just one young person. The rewards are awesome. Invest your time in being an inspiration to a young person.

Darryl continues to support all of my endeavors as evidenced by the letter on the following page I received from him when he learned of a new project I was initiating.

October 10, 2001

To: Whom it may concern

This is a letter of reference for Sandy Rodgers, President/CEO of Nu Vision Enterprises. I had the opportunity to work with Sandy when Nu Vision was based in Los Angeles. I witnessed her build the company from and with nothing more than an idea. Nu Vision became a bright spot in a community that has had its share of tough times. It was a place young people and adults could go and spend time bettering themselves, including me. With Sandy's guidance, I learned a sense of responsibility and how to serve as a leader.

Nu Vision is where I learned how to really believe in myself. Sandy taught me as well as others, that with hard work and determination, a person could accomplish anything they set out to. I'm doing exactly what I want to with my life; serving people as a television news broadcaster.

If there is one thing I have learned about Sandy, it is that she is a person who gets the job done. As long as I have known her she has accomplished every goal she set. She is a compassionate, confident and determined woman; an asset to anyone she comes in contact with.

Yours truly,

Darryl Hood
Anchor/Reporter Fox 5 News
KVVU Broadcasting Corporation
Henderson, Nevada

Aubrey Boone

Aubrey is actually my nephew by marriage but has become more like a son than any other type of relative.

Aubrey and Malcolm were raised together in California as cousins. Over the years their bond has become closer than most brothers have. They each know they can depend on the other when no one else is around. I appreciate the special bond and love that have grown between each of them.

Aubrey visited Malcolm frequently when he first started at Morehouse. Malcolm had no relatives in Atlanta, so Brey (as he is called by family) was constantly travelling to Atlanta to be with him.

Aubrey is a very loving spirit. Growing up in the bitterness of Compton California has stifled him. I have listened to him throughout the years and have come to understand he feels there is no need to plan for a future. A lot of the young men in our inner cities/communities have little if any hope for life after 25! That is sad to me, but its reality for these young men. So even if I can't make a difference in the lives of the thousands that live there, I can make a difference with this one loving soul.

In 1997, Malcolm and I, then sharing a home again in Atlanta received a call that Aubrey had been savagely beaten. He sustained a broken jaw, which had to be wired; lost several teeth; and sustained serious injury to his eyes.

We didn't have all the details, we were both in shock. Neither of us saying a word. I reported out for work and headed straight for my church. I pulled a couple of the men aside, explained what had happened and we all went into prayer. Brey was seriously injured, unconscious and barely hanging on. We maintained a prayer vigil until he was released. I thank God for Aubrey's life!

Aubrey stays with me now, the majority of the time he visits Atlanta. Usually we are on different time schedules, which prevents sharing and us from talking. One recent visit, however, we had and took advantage of a rare opportunity to converse. There was so much pain in his eyes. He's been let down by society. In his heart and soul Aubrey yearns for more. He deserves the best life has to offer. I want to continue our dialog to give him the opportunity to be heard by someone who loves him unconditionally.

Aubrey has so much wisdom and love to share. I told Pops, Aubrey's grandfather, when I left Los Angeles that I wanted to buy a huge house with lots of room, to provide a home for my nephews and other young men who wanted an escape from a life of negativity. My dream is still unfolding.

I make my modest home available to all of my family. I've housed and entertained two nephews so far at different times.

Aubrey I Love You Very Much. LIFE IS GOOD, ALL THE TIME!!

Note: reach back or forward into the community, into your family - pick someone up. Help someone less fortunate!

GOD WILL SURELY BLESS YOUR EFFORTS......

Bobby Shelton

Bobby's mother, Delora Holmon, and I have been very dear sister friends for over thirty-four years. Bobby is an only, much beloved child. He makes it very easy to love him and we all do. Basically I've known Bobby all of his life.

We have a friendship and not a mother-son type of relationship. Bobby is very wise (see his letter in the first chapter), we would have long talks when I shared the home of his mother during the early 90's. The three of us were uniquely different; each had a different schedule. We often joked there was someone always awake in that house and it was true!

Bobby would compose music for hours. I always wanted to hear what he was working on. For Bobby his success was slow in coming to realization. He kept at it, making changes when necessary. He stayed on course. Musicians have always intrigued me by their creativity. We became supporters of each other's art; I am a clothing designer and mutually respected the talents of each other.

Bobby is an excellent cook. I loved to watch him stir-fry a meal, which is one way I have not mastered. His food was always so tasty, incredibly delicious.

Bobby was a pure blessing for me when I lived with them. I was going through a low opinion of myself period. Bobby didn't intrude in my personal affairs. When people love you however, they can only remain mute for so long.

Bobby was concerned with the discrepancy in what I was saying and what I was doing. He criticized the personal relationship I was involved in at the time. A man he felt unworthy of my love and affection. Bobby would have a room-brightening smile on his face throughout our discussion. I knew in my heart he was completely correct. I did not have the inner strength to terminate the relationship. I was clinging to someone. Eventually the time came when the man I had been dating decided he wanted out. I was forced out of a situation I had no business being in. I locked myself in my bedroom for three days. I don't think Bobby left home the entire time. When I finally emerged he was there with words of comfort and encouragement. I thank God for Bobby; he was my comforter during a dark valley experience.

Craig Kevin Butler

My niece, Nona, referred me to Craig when I needed a new hair stylist. Nona and Craig were good friends and had gone to cosmetology school together.

Craig became my new stylist. Nu Vision had recently moved into its new facility on Vermont Avenue in Los Angeles. As Craig and I discussed our dreams I discovered Craig dreamed of being in his own salon. There just happened to be a shop next door to Nu Vision and the owner Harry, was looking for someone to manage the beauty salon.

Harry was a barber. I gave Craig the information, made the introductions with the two of them. Shortly thereafter, Craig opened his own salon next door to Nu Vision!

I watched with pride as Craig remodeled the salon, purchased equipment and advertised his new business.

Craig became extremely active with Nu Vision, we were within walking distance, actually only a wall separated us. Craig was the company's stylist and was featured at each of our fashion shows. Craig desired to become more active and ultimately organized the men's department of Nu Vision – For Men Only. FMO became a vital component of Nu

Vision and addressed critical issues for men.

Craig and I would spend time together strategizing our respective businesses and their expansion. We attended and graduated from a small business economic development course. We were so proud of ourselves for having completed the course, not everyone that started had the fortitude to finish, and it was an extensive course. We were provided with valuable information and tools to manage our businesses.

Craig and I had Bible Study daily; sharing scripture and lessons with each other. God was an integral part of our relationship and our businesses. We were members of different Churches and denominations. At one location or the other one could always find us discussing the sermons or Bible lesson we had heard. There was not a specific amount of time, much time as we could spend we would take. Prayer opened all meetings and rehearsals. We prayed all the time, seeking God's wisdom and guidance.

Craig's mother openly welcomed me into the family. Sharing her son freely with me. Being business neighbors and becoming closer, we spent more time together than with anyone else in our lives.

I received a call Craig had been rushed to the emergency room, suffering with a tumor on the base of his neck. I was there immediately, my son needed me. His mom, girlfriend and me stood watch over Craig.

I assisted with handling his business affairs. It was a very frightening experience. Didn't know how the tumor would affect his hand or head movement or range of motion. Recovery seemed to last forever. I missed my friend, my son, my business associate, and my Bible study partner. Thanks God for complete healing!

Craig had unresolved issues with his father. There were questions Craig felt, demanded an answer to. The unanswered questions began to have a negative influence on Craig. He had a son and did not desire to make the same mistakes he felt his father had made with him. He became obsessed with getting an answer from his father.

In vain, Craig relentlessly sought the answers he desperately needed to know. I could sense his rage, his anger. We discussed this challenge frequently. I attempted to explain that he couldn't force his father to quote the answers, as he wanted to hear them. When the time was right, his father would answer. I reminded Craig to be opened to how his father answered, because it would probably not sound the way he wanted it. At the time I left Los Angeles, Craig had not received the answers he was searching for.

Craig was my personal stylist. My hair was always professionally styled and well cared for. I had a standing weekly appointment but went to him as often as I needed, especially if an important meeting was approaching.

Craig remains my friend forever. He still does my hair when I visit Los Angeles. Craig has expanded his business, adding more stylists and remodeled the salon.

Craig married his love, two years after I left Los Angeles. They have a beautiful home and raising a wonderful family. My prayers remain with Craig and his family.

Note: encourage people to pursue their dreams. Offer support and assistance. Praise them along the way. Keep God in the mix!!

Craig I Love You and know without question you are seeking your truth. I bless you as you journey through life. Thanks for sharing so much of your life with me.

Damen Fletcher

I met Damen when he became a model with Ubitquitdus Modeling Company. His Mother, Betty, was a major contributor to the company's huge success.

Damen is a natural performer. He loved modeling and excelled in school. Damen has extended his talents to include studies in tap and acting. He was forever involved in competitions across the nation. I attended to support him as much as I could.

Betty provided all the opportunities a child could possibly want in life to her youngest son. Damen has remained respectfully appreciative to his mother for supporting him throughout his experimental stages of growth. Damen has blessed his mother by always excelling!

It was a pleasure to have a student like Damen up on stage demonstrating the skills that had been taught during the classes. Damen simply flowed with the motion, in sync naturally with all the routines. He was just a marvel on stage.

As you can tell I sincerely appreciated his talents and dedication to perfecting his skills.

Malcolm was Damen's idol. So when Malcolm chose Morehouse College in Atlanta, Betty and I both knew that's where Damen would want to go also. Damen did attend Morehouse but his passion remained in the performing arts.

After much deliberation, he returned to Los Angeles to continue with what he feels is his calling in life. I commend Damen for the courage to follow his dream and not be pressured by the goals of any other. Damen I knew it took a great deal of strength, and I am proud of you for remaining focused on your calling. You just come to life on stage. I know you will be constantly blessed by being a blessing to others on stage.

Damen is making his acting debut in June 2002 on the FX show 'The Shield".
DAMEN I LOVE YOU SON. KEEP REACHING UP!

Ricky Winters

I first met Ricky at Circuit City; we worked together in the Atlanta Home Delivery warehouse.

Ricky became my first adopted son in Atlanta. We talked and hung out together all the time. It was at Ricky's home where the idea of me doing a men's ministry was first discussed. I am indebted to Ricky for being instrumental in the writing of this book.

It was the day after a Championship Title Boxing match that the idea was conceived. I had walked over to Ricky's apartment; we lived in the same complex. We were sitting around talking about the fight with a couple of his friends. As the discussion developed into another session of me ministering to young men, his friend Chou replied "You should do more of this. You have really helped me out with your wisdom." I was indeed flattered but recognized I did have a gift, a special gift of communicating with young men.

When I met Ricky's mother, Dora, on a visit to Atlanta from Indianapolis she asked me to please watch over her son. It was funny because she was not the first woman to ask me to help with their son. But Ricky wasn't as young as my other adopted sons. It was strange to hear a big, full-grown man call me Ma! And when Malcolm was first introduced to Ricky he didn't like the fact that as he put it, "He's too old to be calling you his mother!!" There was a few years difference in their ages. Malcolm never had a problem with anyone calling me their mother before then.

Actually several of his friends had called me Mom during the years. Most of them were advised directly by Malcolm to call me Mom. Somehow this was different and Malcolm was not too thrilled! All of that changed over the course of time.

Malcolm and Ricky started referring to each other as brothers. The three of us would go on shopping trips together.

Ricky and I hung out all the time; shopping, going out, comparing recipes and sampling each other's food. At the clubs the men vying for my attention had to measure up to

Ricky's inspection, and he was very strict on them.

Ricky is an excellent cook. I had advised him to follow his dream of opening his own restaurant. Ricky has yet to pursue his dream. Someday we will all be blessed to eat at Ricky's Place. Until then I enjoy his cooking as often as I can.

We would both become so wide open with deep hidden concerns. Each allowed ourselves to be completely honest with the other. Receiving positive criticism can be unsettling, but it was a time to be truthful. All falsehood banished, each fear overcome one by one by being naked with another in conversation. Naked meaning no covering, no protection, nothing to stand in the way of truly communicating.

Somehow, somewhere Ricky felt lost. Felt lowly of himself at the deepest level. On the surface it did not show.

Here I am exposing it, only because he has grown so much by recognizing his own self-worth. I am sure Ricky would welcome me sharing his story so others can learn and grow from it.

Ricky was chasing love, not just looking for it. He fell in love quickly, almost overnight. I remember him talking with a young lady on the phone that I had introduced him to. The next thing I knew he had proposed! Never met her, had not talked with her for a long time. So we went into therapy! I desperately wanted Ricky to discover what made him so preoccupied with 'looking for love'.

Instead of finding love or even getting close he was chasing women away from him. During the months that followed Ricky began to recognize and accept his own self, with all the flaws and goodness. He stopped chasing love; he focused on loving himself unconditionally. Regardless if he called it a mistake, a stupid thing to do or some other form of negative criticism he accepted it, what he had done. He learned how to change his self-talk, how he used his self-talk. He was more gentle with himself; stopped beating himself up constantly.

I became part of Ricky's extended family, everyone knew me in his family. And Ricky was an integral part of my family. He and my father became close friends; my dad even had two African outfits custom made for him. Ricky did most of the cooking for Malcolm's college graduation celebration. We were there for each other when needed.

In 1996, I was working out of town and my dog had gotten seriously ill, there was Ricky to take us to the Vet. That's only one account, there are dozens more. This is just to illustrate the bond we had.

A few years ago, Ricky and JoJuan found each other. Ricky became the first adopted son to have healed and moved forward to the next step. He was now prepared to handle LOVE.

Had taken the steps to be a stronger individual, possessing higher self-esteem and self-love. Malcolm, Derrius – Malcolm's son- and I were all a part of the beautiful wedding ceremony celebrating the union of Mr. and Mrs. Winters. As with all couples, they have encountered challenges, thank God they work through the issues as they surface. Jo Juan thank you for loving my son Ricky.

Ricky, I LOVE YOU! I am indeed pleased with your growth spiritually and emotionally. You have so much to offer to this world. May God continue to bless you with the fortitude to keep seeking the Best for you and your family.

Love You, MA

Clarence Richardson

Clarence was my supervisor at Denny's Restaurant and became my second adopted son. Clarence and I would engage in very serious discussions about life, relationships, politics and religions. All the subjects one would normally shy away from especially between boss and worker. The other servers would sometimes dislike our talking because Clarence would pull me off the floor to talk. He was another soul that just needed to be heard. Talking with Clarence wasn't always easy.

I really had to stretch, call on all the patience of the Universe to talk with Clarence. In the beginning I would just walk away from him, insisting I had to get back to work, he was my supervisor! Clarence was indeed the most verbal of any of my sons, and that is no small accomplishment.

Through that tough guy exterior there was an individual searching for truth. Clearance's questions were sometimes difficult to hear, let alone engage in discussion.

But he was relentless in seeking me out. I had to pray to God for guidance, for me to have the right words to say to him. Of course God answered my prayer requests.

But I frequently ended discussions with Clarence by walking away, shaking my head. I knew and accepted I had been hired by Denny's for a reason other than just employment. I did love working with the customers and this was a new working experience for me. I had always worked in an office environment, My lesson and blessing was to become a close friend to Clarence.

Clarence, too, was experiencing difficulties in personal relationships. Chasing and running off women. Clarence was not looking for love, just women. Although our conversations seldom focused on interpersonal relationships, I had to explore this subject with him. It took time to develop this area.

Clarence would challenge my beliefs and understanding of scripture. We would spend hours on scripture, I would stay after my shift was finished or Clarence would come in on his day off. Clarence grew up believing and fully accepting women did not belong in the pulpit. My Minister was Rev. Dr. Barbara Lewis King, founder of Hillside Chapel and Truth Center. Clarence had an extremely difficult time with accepting that fact. He refused to attend church with me. I believe it was fear that prevented him from attending. Fear that what he had been indoctrinated with may be incorrect, that women could be effective and efficient leaders of a church.
I do not have confrontations with people about their religious beliefs. I will

discuss if the conversation can be open and
both can share in the input. Clarence never
attempted to persuade me to leave Hillside.
He settled with being curious about women
ministries. It's ironic that he often
referred to me as a Minister. So there was
some acceptance on his part. As we reached a
mutual respect for each other's views we
began addressing the other areas, especially
his dealings with women, which were high
concern for me.

Clarence admitted his inappropriate
behaviors and started working to improve his
relationships. He basically stopped
collecting women and began understanding the
reasons why he had indulged in such
behavior. Clarence settled down and worked
on himself. Set limits, established
boundaries for his relationships. Clarence
began to have healthy relationships with
women.

And now my second adopted son was engaged.
Clarence asked me to be his Best (Wo) Man. I
was immensely honored. I had never been a
Best Man! When I first met Erica, his
fiancée at the time, he had told her if I
didn't approve of her he would have to call
off the wedding. I remember she was so
nervous. When I found out what had been said
I slapped Clarence on his head. Clarence is
indeed blessed to have a beautiful wife.
Erica loves Clarence; they have a gorgeous
daughter, Carmen Rene. She's my other
granddaughter.

Clarence would sometimes call me his mother,
then his sister, then back to mother.
Regardless of the title - I love Clarence
unconditionally. I welcome our debates and
lengthy discussions.

I Love You. Stay true to yourself. TRUST
GOD….

Carlos Madkins

Carlos was number three adopted son, in
Atlanta. I was newly hired with Airborne
Express working as the driver check- in
Agent. Carlos was one of the drivers.

Carlos and I became friends and we talked
all the time. He would come into the tiny
office I worked in, sit on the floor or on
top of boxes. It didn't matter to him. Often
Carlos would fall asleep on the floor in the
office.

We talked about life, goals and dreams.
Carlos reminded me of my own son, their
facial features and physical build were
similar. Carlos soon began calling me his
mother. Everyday, without fail, Carlos could
be found near or in my office.

Since I left that particular station Carlos
and my son have become good friends. Carlos
was there to help me move, twice!

Carlos has progressed steadily since leaving
Airborne. He has an excellent Manager
position with a prestigious Corporation. He
got married to Keisha; they have two
beautiful sons and another child on the way.
They have a wonderful newly built home south
of Atlanta.

I don't talk with Carlos as often as I do my
other sons. He's doing very well and I am
extremely proud of him.

Carlos, I LOVE YOU.

Lesson: spend quality time talking and listening. Sharing wisdom and insights is useful to an individual's positive growth. Serving our fellow human is our purpose for living.

Terrance LaCount

Terrance is the last of my adopted sons who have healed the necessary wounds and is involved in an exclusive relationship. The fourth in seven years.

Terrance and I started as co-workers at Airborne Express. He was the Independent Contractor supervisor and I was the Airborne supervisor. I was solely responsible for one of the country's heaviest outbound operations. I could not have been successful without the full support of the Contractors. Terrance never failed me in that regard. He helped me with learning the best strategies in overcoming the many and various obstacles I would encounter. Terrance is a true, genuine comic. And I love to laugh. We bonded instantly. But it took time before we became close personal friends. Terrance's wit is surely stage material.

Terrance is a very intelligent and wise young man. Terrance is very protective of me. Terrance is very dear to me, most people recognize and accept it.

Terrance's mother died while he was in college. I became Terrance's surrogate mother and close friend. I took the responsibility of being a surrogate mother very seriously. We shared every opportunity we had. We would talk for hours on the phone. During our conversations we discovered we possessed the same qualities and held the same views on most subjects. Most discussions included, if not totally centered on an individual's drive and ambition. Terrance held a high level of self-esteem and self-love. He desired more of life than most people dare dreamed. He constantly works to improve himself in all areas - emotionally, mentally, physically, spiritually and financially. Terrance would have difficulty accepting that other young people did not have the same aspirations. So we concluded to share our thoughts and philosophies with each other. And this is the single most important reason we talked endless hours.

Terrance has such keen insights for an individual his age. His mother took special care in raising her children, especially her youngest son.

Terrance complained of not being able to find a woman with similar qualities and goals. Would often say none existed. When Terrance discovered he was attracting to himself what he held in his consciousness, he deliberately began to change his self-talk. He stopped dating just to be dating. He wanted a woman of substance.

Terrance felt I was guilty of not demanding exactly what I wanted in a man. Terrance has always been very blunt with what he said to me. He is perhaps more protective than my own son. He did not tolerate anyone disrespecting me. So when it came to the man I would date, his expectations were higher than mine were. He demanded more of me than I was demanding of myself. Terrance helped to keep me true to myself.

He respected the times that I spent in reflection; he never rushed me to discuss any aspect that he felt I was working through. And when I came to him he already knew what I was challenged with. He always read me so well.

Terrance had an unresolved issue with his stepfather. He felt abandoned by him after his mother died. The feeling was eating away at him; he did not like to discuss it. He held onto negative feelings until recently. After many debates and true sharing Terrance has decided to forgive his stepfather. He has accepted his need to release the situation with love. Healing can now occur for him.

Terrance thank you for being brave, courageous and willing to let go and let God. So often we hold onto feelings because somewhere along the way we accepted it makes us powerful over the situation. But as Terrance has discovered the power goes to the situation when we refuse to release it with complete love and forgiveness. Recently Terrance had an accident that damaged his shoulder. He told me the incident provided him a whole new insight on his life and vulnerability.

After many more discussions and him joining me at Hillside where he heard Dr. Na'im Akbar speak, Terrance understands a man's worth is not determined by his muscles and prowess but by his heart. That was such a wonderful revelation for Terrance.

His whole perspective on life changed as a result of his shoulder surgery and the sermon Dr. Akbar gave. Terrance and I had talked about him joining me at church; this particular Sunday was his first visit to Hillside. As I told Terrance it was all done in Divine time and order. I had been telling Terrance for a few months about my history with my adopted sons. We both laughed because there was not a single prospect visual for him at the time. I assured him it was going to happen, he would find his soul mate and get married. That made Terrance nervous. Never in my wildest dreams did I expect for it to unfold the way it has.

His soul mate just happened to be a very fine young lady that I had served as a mother to over the last four years.
Lorraine and I were very close. We also spent hours talking, on the phone and in person. This was Terrance's match! It was shocking in the beginning, as their relationship was building I spent less and less time with both. No more dinners with Terrance, something we did as often as we could. No more long hours discussing our views on life with either of them. I was lonely but I knew it was destined to happen. Terrance. I am very proud of you. Stay true to yourself and your convictions. Trust God in all you do.

Know that I love you unconditionally! Stay strong in heart! Love all of life, its all good all the time!

LOVE SANDY

*The greatest miracle of the world Is how two
microscopic Organisms can create A Life!!*

*To feel life growing in the womb.
To witness the birth of that new life!*

God is Awesome

Sandy Rodgers

Written April 1977

To My Son: Malcolm Jerome Tyson

To you, my son, with all the love
I can give to you

You grew inside of me for nine months

I loved you from the very moment I
Discovered I was carrying you

You are my true delight

I love your funny ways
Your determination
Your expressions

My love for you can never die
Just grow deeper

Being instrumental in your development
Is my greatest desire

A Mother's love is more complex
And deeper than any other known
To mankind

For you, my son, I wish all the
Love - Life can give!

Written May 20, 1985
By Malcolm Tyson

Mom, I think that you are Supermom. Because you are sweet and kindness sticks out from all of your love. I can't bear a minute without looking at your beautiful face. If someone would give me all the money in the whole wide world for me not to see or call you, I wouldn't take it.

Malcolm Jerome Tyson

My Beloved Son - My Gift From God!

It took three years for me to become pregnant. Jeff and I did everything we knew, then we asked other people who offered a wide variety of suggestions. Finally we went to the fertility clinic.

I had taken my temperature to determine my ovulation, charted it and reported the results. I worried poor Dr. Hershey every month, told him my family had a history of having menstrual cycles after they had conceived. And every month Dr. Hershey said the same thing - not yet!

Finally Jeff said enough is enough. I was sad and disappointed but he was absolutely correct, I had probably stressed him out too. So I stopped obsessing about becoming pregnant. Cursed the loop and the pills, the contraceptives I had used previously. I agreed with my husband and stopped driving everybody crazy.

I went back to College, to finish what I had started years before. I simply decided to change my entire focus. I even changed my major to Business. I lost about fifty pounds. Within a very short time my periods had stopped.

I had finally gotten pregnant! I was the happiest pregnant woman I have ever known. I glowed the full nine months. I was so happy to be pregnant.

Dr. Weiss calculated according to what I told him my baby would be born mid September. That date came and went. I started walking; I did everything anyone told me to help induce labor. Nothing worked.

I became the proud mother of Malcolm Jerome Tyson on October 28, 1975.

As a baby I would not allow anyone to speak in 'baby talk' around my son. I knew it sounded like crazy talk to me. I did not want my child confused about the language he would first hear. The grand parents, all six of them, thought I was over protective but they honored my request.

I did not allow my son to be confined in a playpen. It just reminded me of a miniature jail cell. One of the grandmothers would not honor that request. Thought it was the only way to watch a child.

Malcolm was not permitted to go back until she agreed not to place him in it. I was in labor three and a half days, tough painful labor! Anyone who could not follow my instructions simply were not allowed to babysit. It did not matter who they were.

Children need room to grow not be restricted or confined. There were certain goals I had for my son.

During his first year of life I accomplished my first goal; taking pictures each month on the 28th to show his stages of development; Malcolm traveled on all major methods of transportation – he flew on an airplane, traveled by car and bus, had taken a train ride and rode on a boat. These were things he would probably not remember, they were my goals nonetheless.

Jeff and I divorced when Malcolm was still a young child, he was only two. I insisted no one spoke negatively about his father in his presence.

I had been exposed to bitter language about my own father all of my life and could not allow it to be repeated. I constantly told Malcolm he had the best father on earth. He called his dad every week also. Jeff was a good father to his son. Jeff spent quality time with Malcolm regularly and provided for him financially.

I wanted my child exposed to as much positive activity as possible. As a young boy he participated in the Boy Scouts, took Harp lessons, Karate lessons and modeling.

The most important element I wanted to depart to Malcolm was the best possible education.

Malcolm's primary education years were spent at New Life Christian School. He was allowed to blossom at his own pace. Malcolm skipped the second grade. By the time he graduated from the sixth grade he was completing ninth grade work successfully.

He was Salutatorian of his sixth grade class. I am eternally grateful to the full teaching team of New Life Christian School for instilling in Malcolm a solid educational foundation.

Because Malcolm was so advanced in studies, a lot of his next six years in school would be repeat work. His Junior High School was located next to a junk yard. One of the teachers made a reference comparing the students' minds and future to that of the junk yard I was furious!

I taught Malcolm to always speak his mind in the most respectful way he could or don't say anything at all. I would speak at that point for him.

Malcolm began high school at a local school. During one of his modeling performances it was announced he was a National Merit Scholar. The principal of Los Angeles Center for Enriched Studies- L.A.C.E.S., a prominent magnet school was in attendance.

Malcolm soon began classes at L.A.C.E.S., with much assistance and persistence from the principal. In transferring him from the local high school, I had to meet with Malcolm's counselor to get his transcripts and released.

The Counselor had the audacity to tell me, a parent, my child would never amount to much, why was I wasting my time. I was so appalled at that educational system.

The Principal at the local high school took no action for that very inappropriate statement by one of his counselors. It took all I had to walk away without creating too much of a disturbance!

Our children were being exposed to individuals who could not elevate their own consciousness, so they picked on the innocent minds of the students. I was so thankful to get Malcolm away from that school.

To Mr. Counselor who desired to misplace his own hellish self-esteem, I say my son graduated from Paramount High School with honors. Malcolm entered Morehouse College in August 1992 in Atlanta Georgia at age sixteen!

I have always instilled in my son and all other youngsters - YOU CAN BE WHATEVER YOU WANT TO BE! Malcolm credits his accomplishments to the repetition of that phrase throughout his formative years.

Parents - we MUST monitor what our children are being fed intellectually and emotionally. Children can learn positive affirmations or believe an untruth about their capabilities.

I urge you, all adults; mentor a child with positive expectations. Their belief in themselves is what determines their future!

At some point Malcolm began calling me 'Larry". I do not remember how it happened or when it started. Everyone would just ask him to repeat himself and when he would say it again, they would just laugh. Even cards and letters were sent to 'Larry'. It was really very special.

My last goal for my son was to graduate from College, which he did in 1996 at age twenty. I was the proudest parent at the graduation. I then released him to do whatever he chose to do with his life. He had done absolutely everything I had requested of him.

My Dad was constantly impressed that Malcolm called whenever he traveled out of town. My dad would say most kids don't do that for their parents living in the same household, Malcolm is thousands of miles away!

I taught Malcolm responsibility early in his life. I was a single parent and we needed to operate as a team. By age eight, Malcolm could cook; wash and iron his clothes.

Later I taught him how to repair his clothes and shop for groceries. He learned how to budget his money by lessons of his allowances running out before the week ended. I told him he should be an asset if he were to get married later in life.

Malcolm has been an entrepreneur most of his life; Cutting grass, washing cars. Part time sales in my dress shop, maintaining a student emergency supply store at College and operating a daycare center.

I am extremely proud of the Man my son has become. His cherished values are hard worker, does not hit females, financially astute, wise and honest. He is very trustworthy.

Malcolm has experienced his fair share of life's challenges. I was always there for him. Not oblivious to what was going on; I trusted how I had raised my son. I love my son unconditionally as I do his beautiful wife, Kenya and my two grandchildren, Derrius and Deja.

Malcolm has been wise most of his life. At age four when my brother, Rudy, died we adults were all very emotional and crying. Perhaps to a child acting rather silly.

One night as we lay in bed he said, "Mama why is everybody crying? They should be happy that Uncle Rudy is in heaven with God". As I shared that statement with the family the crying diminished considerably.

As Malcolm face life challenges he remains a responsible individual. He has been taught to be independent, especially in his thinking. He still reads to improve himself. He has mentored several young men and continues to have an open door for those seeking self-improvement.

Malcolm is a normal young adult. He is a responsible adult. Malcolm is my gift from God. My gratitude was demonstrated by offering my son the best life has.

TRUE UNCONDITIONAL LOVE CONSISTENTLY WITHOUT LIMITS......

We have a mutual love and respect for each other.

Each appreciative of the other.

The following was written by Malcolm in November 2001, somewhere around Thanksgiving.

If I could have chosen a mother, I would have chosen you.
Just wanted to say thank you for the numerous things that you help my family out with. From the conversations on how to go to the potty, to helping me raise a man, to helping my wife grow, to always being there for support when I need an open ear to hear me out.

Thanks you for always being the backbone of our family. We will always be grateful for your enduring heart.

I hope I can live up to your expectations of what a real man is.

My Little Men

- nephews and grandsons

*   *   *

Although not all of my extended or immediate
family are blood relatives, I make no
difference in the love I give to them.
We are all family - full, whole, half, step,
in-law or whatever. Really it's just all
FAMILY!

And they are not all little!

Tony

Anthony King - Tony - AK, that's my nephew. He's my oldest nephew therefore we have a stronger bond than I have with the others. He's more than my nephew he's my friend, business associate and spiritual comrade.

Describing my relationship with AK, just the thought, the anticipation brings a smile to my face and heart. He is genuinely unique and has lived his life on his terms for as long as I can remember.

AK is an extraordinary performer. I am his biggest Fan. Whenever I attend one of his performances, you would not make a mistake in recognizing or hearing me. I'll be the one yelling the most, giving standing ovations and screaming 'That's my nephew!'

And AK performs just for me when I see him on stage. He describes himself as a self created, self developed performer/artist. He has never taken any professional lessons. He simply allows his natural talents to manifest itself, be it during a live performance or in a recording studio. He is awesome.

AK started performing as a child doing the popular 'Pop Lock' dance. And Tony was the best, he was always practicing, always perfecting his steps, his routine. Even at an early age he understood discipline in achieving one's goals. Tony gives totally of himself in all of his endeavors.

His raw, unabashed uniqueness is shared openly and freely. Doubt in his abilities, fear of not succeeding never stopped him. He just keeps going forward towards his aspirations. I've learned the meaning of tenacity by watching AK.

AK calls me his favorite Aunt but he calls each of us his favorite. I appreciate the compliment and whenever we communicate I feel I am the favorite, at least during those precious moments.

AK travels a lot and we live on opposite coasts of the United States. Those few, special moments that we do get to talk lasts for hours. It's as if we just spoke the day before. AK and I are forever connected, always on the same path, the same wave length. As we talk we paraphrase the thoughts and feelings of each other. A spiritual connectedness best describes the vibrations between us.

AK is a wise old, young man. He's an accomplished author and national speaker in addition to his musical talents.

He has produced several CD's of his music. As stated previously, AK willingly displays his raw talent. This is particularly true in his writing. His first book, 'Diary of a Mind and Soul…I AM NOT A MISTAKE' was self published by him.

What I mean by 'raw' is exhibited in the writings in this book, it is unrefined. AK gives you what he's got to deliver to humanity in his style. He refuses to 'dress it up', make sure it's politically correct or deviate from his style. Which explains why he self produced all of his music and his book.

AK lives by his set of ethical standards, which are very high. He tells it like he sees or feels it, period end of story. AK is courageous to the point of completely accepting his talents and sharing them, without apology.

AK stands firm in his convictions in his personal life as well. I have never personally witnessed him disrespect any person. I have seen him stand firm on his views. And some have labeled that disrespectful due to their self imposed fear of exposing their true identity.

I respect and hold AK up in the highest regard for always being brave and bold with his life. AK is married to a very beautiful and talented woman, Rebecca. My nephew loves her without doubt. Rebecca brings out the best in my nephew! As if he needed any coaching.

At Nu Vision Modeling and Entertainment, AK provided assistance in the development of the entertainment segment. He brought in well known and respected artists such as David Whitfield and other cast members of **Lawd Have Mercy,** to rehearse. He gave freely of himself and his resources in helping to build the company.

AK is extremely outspoken. He discusses his issues directly with the individual(s) involved. No one can ever accuse him of gossiping or spreading rumors behind their back. AK does not operate that way. I learned integrity through his actions.

AK and I have discussed many subjects. I feel the one issue most dear to him is the passing on of male wisdom.

It was lacking for him and it left him
somewhat bitter. The sharing, the
unconditional love of the elder men is very
important to our young men. Whatever fears
or failures an elder may harbor does not
excuse them from their duty of 'passing it
on'. In essence we all will sooner or later
define our own lives and destiny, wisdom
from the elders is always needed and
welcomed.

Tony although the absence of unconditional
fatherly love has not deterred you from your
dreams, I pray the issue has been resolved
completely for you and within you.

As one of the elders of this family, even
though I'm a female, allow me to say, I AM
VERY PROUD OF YOU, AS A MAN, AN ARTIST, A
POSITIVE SPIRITUAL SOUL, A TEACHER AND ROLE
MODEL!

I LOVE YOU,
AUNTY SANDY

Munir

I remember when Munir was born. I would love
to just sit and hold him. He accompanied me
as often as possible on outings. Bur Munir
was a baby suffering with sever colic. I
felt so much compassion for him. Nothing
seemed to bring about relief - So he cried a
lot and I would attempt to soothe him.

Munir outgrew the condition but not without
plenty of sleepless nights for his parents
and other caregivers.

I remember Munir as being a rather shy
child. Serious and quiet: A contemplating

spirit; Quietly exploring all of life. His nature has remained mostly unchanged. Nonchalant!

As a young adult, conversations with Munir can be lengthy. He can go for long periods of time just saying hi. Suddenly when you talk with him expecting for the conversation to be brief, he'll go the depths of subjects in talking with you. You never know what mood Munir will be in.

I appreciate the intellectual growth. It seems as if overnight my baby became a grown man. As elders in a family, we need for the children to stay younger longer, perhaps it's our own attempt to remain young.

I expect and anticipate great accomplishments from my nephew. I believe there is the making of a Noble Prize recipient in Munir for a cure, some research or discovery which will significantly impact all of humankind. He is on a mission not yet determined. Perhaps his contributions will be artistic, maybe scientific or philosophical. Regardless of his chosen field of endeavor, I will support and encourage him.

Munir has recently graduated Magnum Cum Laude from Prairie View University in Texas.

I AM EXTREMELY PROUD OF YOU, MUNIR! I LOVE YOU ALWAYS.

Abdur-Raheen

Abdur-Raheen has the same build as his dad, small and strong. He is very sociable. Enjoys the company of other people; never encountering a stranger. He is a very loving individual.

In his older years Abdur-Raheen has become quite a gentleman. Extremely neat in appearance. Debonair. Has a flair about himself. A certain sophistication. A real charmer in the most appropriate and respectful way.

Abdur-Raheen is adventurous about life. Exploring all the wonders life has to offer. He has a wide range of interests such as music; particularly oldies with a special concentration in the Jazz legends; Karate, he has earned several belts and competed in numerous competitions. He has worked for the Ft. Worth Art Museum for the past three years and serves as a life guard along with other responsibilities at the Y. All this while completing College at University of Texas, Arlington. He enjoys traveling also.

I love Abdur-Raheen's life-style, uniquely his own. Very real, very caring, mature and settled. He is a student of life. Eloquent in speech. Smooth and easy interactions with people.

I love you Abdur-Raheen. I pray you are blessed with all your heart can conceive. You are so gifted and special.

Rudy

This time my nephew. Named after an Uncle he never got the opportunity to share life with, named appropriately.

Rudy has lived a full life in his brief life time. He's more than a survivor, he is a conqueror. Rudy is brave, independent and strong. Possess a hearty laugh and broad smile.

Rudy's parents were two loving souls that joined in matrimony while still plagued with enormous negative emotions. Each a beautiful and kind person separately. Together, however, a dangerous liaison, at best. His young life, the early care free days, were interrupted by turmoil.

The violence eroded their family life. His parents were eventually unable to care for him and his younger brother.

Many unpleasant events led to a divorce and incarceration. The hunger for materialism destroyed the family unit.

He spent several years with his paternal grandparents in Louisiana. An invaluable experience creating lasting memories of a joy filled and carefree youth of living in the country. Great care and a tremendous amount of affection were freely given and received. Rudy still reminisces about fishing with PaPa and other beautiful escapades.

Loved by both parents, a custody battle followed.

The operative word - battle. Rudy was uprooted and moved with his mother, brother and step father to North Carolina. His dad would not allow the battle to be over. His unending love for his sons triggered a successful reversal of custody.

Rudy was on his way back to California.

Rudy has remained determined to live a life full of possibilities and opportunities. Rudy excelled in sports in high school, becoming a star athlete playing football. Rudy maintained superior grades and received several scholarship offers. He is currently attending University of Pennsylvania in Philadelphia.

In summary, it has been his decision to overcome obstacles, to be the role model for his younger siblings. Rudy is a rare commodity among young men. He is constantly respectful and appreciative to everyone who has helped him along his journey.

Rudy you are truly a blessing and inspiration to everyone. I am very proud of all of your victories. Keep the wind at your back as you continue to achieve your dreams and aspirations. I LOVE YOU….

Chantz Jordan

I was there at the hospital when he was born. I was with his mother through most of the pregnancy. He was such a big beautiful, healthy baby. I remember saying 'OUCH'.

My son, Malcolm, adopted him immediately. He was barely four months old and Malcolm was taking Chantz around our neighborhood telling everyone that he was his baby. Those family genes, there was so question because they looked so much alike.

Chantz stayed with us as often as we could get him.

At fifteen months Chantz began his modeling career with Nu Vision Modeling. He made his stage debut at 22 months at one of the biggest Fashion Events of the 90's. Trust me he stole the show!

Chantz usually accompanies me on trips, so his going to Atlanta with me in 1992 was no different. We were escorting Malcolm to college. Chantz and I hung out at the pool or played in the room while the older boys discovered the city.

Chantz was only four when I decided to leave Los Angeles. He has always said amazing phrases. But shortly after I left he had his mother to call me. Chantz said, "Auntie you've been gone so long I almost forgot what you look like". I thought for sure my niece had put him up to saying that, she assured me it was all his idea and wording. I was so touched and I missed him also.

Chantz was raised by his grandfather. Mo was a retired truck driver and baby sat to help out. But, Mo thoroughly enjoyed watching T.V.. So his idea was to keep Chantz on the bed watching T.V. with him. Mo would hold Chantz by the foot to prevent him from crawling off the bed.

In the process Chantz became addicted to T.V. He became totally lost watching the tube, simply lost! He could not concentrate on anything else. Does everything he can to watch T.V., at any cost. Caution: do not rob a child of creativity by sentencing them to television.

His challenge will be to find an appropriate substitute. He is helping his younger brothers with their learning and that certainly helps. Chantz is an excellent student and have experienced playing different sports. His love of music has led him to singing in the choir at church.

Chantz has also written a couple of songs and formed a signing group last summer. He definitely has talent.

Chantz I Love You very much. You can do anything you set your mind to doing. Set your goals high, reach for the stars!!!

Joseph

As a baby we played games together. Jo Jo loved to laugh and play. When he was about three years old, the popular commercial was of a retail store having a sale: customers would be waiting in the darkness of night for the store to open. At the end a woman would be scratching on the door, peering in, saying "Open, Open, Open." This was our favorite re-enactment, play activity. Jo never tired of this game, unlike his Auntie!

Joseph is a very active child with a high level of endless energy. One would get exhausted just watching his vigor, his endurance.

Joseph has a very loving nature, is very helpful. Last summer I was on vacation in Los Angeles with two grandchildren under age six and had picked up two nieces in Texas. I needed to borrow some of Joseph's energy.

Instead I enlisted his assistance. Joseph immediately jumped at the opportunity to help me with the younger children. He was very responsible. I never had to remind him of his duties.

There were two front yards full of playing children. Joseph never let that distract him. When he is given control of a situation, he becomes very serious about what he is charged with doing. All this at age nine.

Allow children to demonstrate their skills in a supportive atmosphere. Our children may surprise us with their abilities.

 To Joseph-
From Open - Open - Open
To Thank You - Thank You - Thank You

I Love You…. Auntie Sandy

Trenton

The youngest son of Thomas and Juandessa, currently my youngest nephew.

Trenton is a little character! And a character he is. Everyone told me he didn't talk when I visited. He was maybe one year old. So I said to Trenton, "If you can't talk to me then I don't know what you want."

Trenton has been talking to me every since. Perhaps I couldn't understand him but he certainly understood what I told him. Prior to that, he would just point and grunt, folks would respond to his gestures. I wouldn't. And he talked to me all the time, Bless his heart!

I returned with my two grandchildren in July of the same year. My granddaughter has a true gift of speaking, complete sentences by the time she was twelve months old.

Deja taught Trenton or perhaps Trenton taught himself to be able to keep up with Deja. Deja was two and Trenton almost nineteen months. That was a real combination of little people. Trenton even began calling me Grandma, after all that's what Deja called me.

Trenton would slip away and whenever he was MIA for long, you must search him out. On one adventure he found my cell phone and called Atlanta. The friend he had called, knew where I was and called on the house phone to tell me, "A little person is on your cell". I found Trenton and he was still talking on my cell. Trenton also made other changes to my cell phone that I couldn't undo!

So when I was advised he was being baptized, I told them he should be DUNKED not sprinkled! He is all boy and I love every ounce of him.

I love Trenton's adventurous nature. He keeps everyone alert.

T.J. (Thomas Michael)

My first time seeing T.J. was on a visit to Los Angeles. My dad had picked me up from the airport. We met my sister, Janice, my niece and her newest son at a buffet type restaurant. I prepared my plate. I told his mother to get her food; I would wait at the table with the baby.

By the time Juandessa returned to the table T.J. had eaten all of my food. I couldn't believe this baby had such an awesome appetite.

Greedy! That feeding experience bonded us immediately. I tried not to eat around him again during my visit - Just kidding.

T.J. is fairly quiet now. Keeps to himself. Doesn't talk a lot. He is very smart and has appeared in several publications, very photogenic.

David

A quiet soul, reserved. Like his father, my youngest brother, I do not really know him. That saddens me as I attempt to write about my relationship with my nephews.

In a lot of ways he is similar to his father, whom he is named after. Mysterious and quiet are the definitive terms for him.

Keyth

Another nephew I haven't taken the time to truly get acquainted with.

Keith is very gifted athletically. He is the second eldest son and very outspoken.

Derrius

My grandson is all boy, a sheer flow of masculine energy. Derrius is very smart, extremely inquisitive, always testing his boundaries since the tender age of six months.

It seems like the first word he spoke was 'Grandma' and as loud as one could stand! I was so thrilled. That was just the beginning. Whenever I traveled I would ask for permission to take Derrius with me. My daughter-in-law had a huge fear of flying, anytime I drove Derrius accompanied me.

Going by airplane was not happening until he was four years old. We always had fun together. The summer of 2001, my grandchildren and I drove across the country. Stopping and staying in Louisiana, Texas, California and Nevada. We were on the road for seven weeks, what an adventure!

This past school year I accepted the responsibility for taking and picking Derrius up from school. This has been quite an eventful year! And an honor to share these most precious moments with him.

Seriously I have grown through this experience. Derrius attends a Christian School and would have questions morning and afternoon. I believe Derrius was more advanced intellectually and had problems staying focused which created behavioral problems.

Monday and Tuesday would be fine but those last three days of the week – well let's just say they weren't as good as the first two. Derrius was spanked to no avail, punished to no avail. We tried everything, nothing seemed to make a difference.

Derrius and I would pray together prior to him getting out of the car. We talked on the way about following all the rules. He knew them all well. I kept talking. The problem continued. Like most children he wanted, needed to blame someone else for his problems. He talked about the devil in him making him do bad.

I would explain God created him good not
evil, there was no devil in him. It took
weeks before he finally accepted his choices
were the culprit for his misbehaving in
school. I even substituted on several days
in his class. They all had so much more
energy than the teacher.

Every morning were discussions detailing his
activities and behaviors. The reports
remained unchanged for Wednesday,
Thursday and Friday. I never gave up on my
children, any of them. I was always seeking
a positive solution.

For myself I recorded a tape of an
affirmation from Iyanla Vanzant's 'Until
Today'. The affirmation was I Am GOOD! I had
followed the suggestion in the book, to
record the affirmation and play it often.

One morning the tape was still in when
Derrius got in the car with me heading for
school. Derrius was surprised to hear
Grandma's voice on the tape. You know coming
from out of the radio speakers.

He began to grin. His eyes got so BIG as he
heard the affirmations. Now every morning I
play the tape upon his request. He is so
smart, he has memorized most of the words
and even imitate the vocal annotations.

Great news, Derrius has maintained good
behavior all week. We are all very happy and
more relaxed especially Derrius.

Sometimes the self improvement methods we use, if chosen carefully, can help our children and Grandchildren.

Children are never too young to saturate their consciousness with Powerful, Self-affirming statements.

Thanks Iyanla!

Derrius, I Love You so very, very much. You are so extremely smart. I know one day you will become great at whatever you decide you want to be.

As of this writing Derrius advised me he wants to be a Policeman, Fireman, ride a motorcycle and one of those big trucks that you see on television (Monster Trucks). He said he will go to College first and then get married. We have had a great year driving back and forth to school.

This is a new incident that has just recently occurred.

The rapid movements of squirrels have intrigued my grandson for years. Derrius was visiting Grandma Toni and asked if he could go to a friends' house just a few doors away. While he was on his way to Marisia's a squirrel caught his attention.

Squirrels are very common in Georgia. They can be seen darting across most yards, dashing across the road and running up trees. The point is they move very quickly. Derrius thought it would be great to have a squirrel as a pet.

So he caught one by the tail because he was going to take it to Grandma's house for her to put in the birdcage so he could have a pet squirrel.

The squirrel was wiggling too much for Derrius' comfort so he decided he would hold it around the middle section. As he grasped the mid section he said "His head turned all the way around so he could look at me."

The squirrel bit into his finger and wouldn't let go! He had to use his other hand to pull it off and threw it to the ground. The Doctors and Nurses at the hospital were amazed, as we all are, that someone had actually caught a squirrel, especially a small boy!

As I stated in the beginning, he is all-boy!! That's my curious grandson. Derrius said it was a baby boy squirrel. Perhaps Derrius will add Veterinarian to his list of occupations or an expert featured on The Animal Planet program.

Family Men

This group of men are all
part of my family. Some by marriage,
some by blood. They are important to me.
I love them each very much.

John Moore

Mo is what we all call him. Mo is my sister, Janice's mate for the last twenty plus years. Mo is very loving and extremely wise. He is much older, chronologically, than my sister yet his heart is younger than his grandchildren – whom he adores.

Mo is my big brother and confidant. He is always willing to listen, he doesn't probe. Mo provides me with his insights and wisdom, as I travel on my journey. Mo has long encouraged me to become a politician. I always thought that was peculiar. He would say I fought so hard for injustices in society that politics just seemed to him a perfect profession for me.

Mo is still close friends with both of my former husbands. They visit him regularly.

Mo enjoys socializing with the younger men in the neighborhood also. Everyone drops by to talk over their problems with Mo. He plays cards, he will play for hours with them, sometimes an entire day.

Mo listens carefully to what is spoken, more importantly, to what is unspoken. The special ingredient with the communication is, he does not repeat what is said to him. That can sometimes trigger the curiosity in my sister, Mo just laughs remaining silent.

Thanks Mo for our endless talks and sharing.

Mo is a graceful dancer and truly enjoys dancing. He would escort a group of ladies out and dance with each of us.
Always a true gentleman and escort.

A few years ago while on vacation to his birth place of Houston Texas, Mo suffered a heart attack. He was hospitalized.

Janice had to return home without him, which was difficult for her. Mo changed! It appeared the illness immobilized him. He became sedentary. This caused concern for all of us. This lively, outgoing, virile man had become a stay at home inactive individual. Over the years his activity has increased by my sister's insistence that he get up and go somewhere. She has created errands just for that purpose.

Mo has been one of my major supporters. It didn't matter what course I decided to take. A favorite saying of his regarding my positive attitude, "She's ready, even if she doesn't get to go." I appreciate the unconditional love displayed to me throughout the years.

I Love You, Mo.

Sherman Gistarb

My cousin has showed me love all my life. So when he came to California fifteen years ago, I assumed he came to visit me. To my surprise and enjoyment his mission was to re-capture the love of his younger years.

That person just happened to be my best friend, Carol. When Sherman discovered Carol was living in Oakland California, off he went! I was so tickled, I had never witnessed that type of demonstrated romantic love.

Sherman is an extremely loving individual. Forever considering the welfare of others over his own needs. So when he was separated from his children during their early childhood, a gigantic hole began to grow in his life, his heart.

Considering their welfare and his relationship with his ex-wife, their mother Sherman decided the best thing to do was for him to leave the state where they lived. I believe he first experienced a long period of denial. Sherman progressed through the other emotions while seeking refuge from his pain. Communication was not in order.

Communication with his children ended. And he suffered silently! And for a man who sincerely enjoys talking, this had to be difficult for him. No communication with the individuals he loved the most.

Sherman is very supporting and nurturing with the women in his life. He spends his vacations with his widowed mother in Louisiana to help around the house and yard.

He just lays in bed talking with her all day and night. Like I said he loves to talk. Sherman loves his family unconditionally.

Sherman, I Love You…

Robert Charles Armstead

I call Charles the wise old man of the family. He remains the mature one. As the elder of his immediate family he takes care of his siblings. He shows concerns, respect, love and encouragement. Charles does the same for each and every member of the extended family as well.

Charles had lived in Los Angeles until a health issue forced him to depart. He relocated in Washington State. One year my son visited and he was so excited when he returned home. Malcolm and Charles had formed a special bond.

Charles is a gracious host and enjoys entertaining. He has remained supportive of my son, especially when he left Los Angeles to attend college in Atlanta. Checking with him constantly on things he needed.

Charles stands ready to share his resources. He will help with business plans or make introductions with one of his many business associates nationwide. Charles is my business mentor. I have solicited his advice in many undertakings, he has a sixth sense with the intricacies of business ownership.

Thanks Charles for being available for me and Malcolm.

Thank you for continually having the time and choosing to share your resources.

I Love You, Sandy

Lloyd Goff

My cousin who has made an indelible mark on Dayton, Ohio.

Forever family centered. Always supportive. And surely always have a hilarious story to share. Just a funny guy.
I was attending a week long training class in Wilmington Ohio and had advised Lloyd. I had no idea how far it was away from Dayton,

Lloyd said it was close. There was my cousin to pick me up as planned.

His brother, Kennon also lived in Dayton. That evening we all went to dinner, Kennon and Rhonda, Lloyd and Roseda and me. We went to a chic restaurant on the lake. Lloyd started telling jokes and stories, they were endless. We were laughing so loudly; you know the kind that brings the laughter and joy right up from your toes through your entire body. It did not matter, there was no time to be stiff or uncomfortable.

The other guests in this packed restaurant probably applauded as we left, just kidding. Perhaps it had a wonderful impression on them and they each found something to brighten their day, lighten their load. I had a great time. Thanks Cuz.

Lloyd is an accomplished businessman. Breaking records with his Gas/convenience Store in the inner city of Dayton.

He has a respectable non-alcoholic establishment. He knows his customers and calls them by name. He immediately reacts to all customer concerns. His employees respect him also. Lloyd is a shining star in an otherwise dismal location in Dayton.

He has recaptured the spirit of a neighborhood business. Respect is mutual between him, his employees and customers.

Thanks Lloyd for having the vision and courage to be successful! Thanks for being a role model in the community.
You are truly a very spirited individual.

I Love You.

Thomas Johnson

I've known Thomas for about twenty years, first met him when he was just barely a teenager. He was dating my niece.

Today, Thomas calls me his favorite Auntie. He is married to my niece/daughter Juandessa. I had already moved to Atlanta when they began dating again. I am very protective of my niece and know she only deserves the very Best in life.

Thomas honestly loves his wife, my niece. To witness the love between them, shared with their children I know all is well. Thomas is a wonderful father. Thomas sincerely loves Juandessa.

For some reason or other, there were so many outside people invading their relationship. On a recent visit I witnessed how too many well meaning busy bodies can disturb the calm flow, momentum. Thomas stood his ground, as if he should have had to prove a point to anyone other than his wife.

Accusations were flying rampant.
Disagreements with outsiders who thought they had a right to direct their marriage. It was wild! And it seemed the numbers of intruders were growing daily. It was more than I could stand or understand. Thomas remained devoted to his wife and family. They sought spiritual counsel. They are working through the challenges that life and living sometimes hands all of us. They are doing it together.

Thomas has not accepted his genius, his power. He is a very warm and caring man; a nurturing individual.

Thomas is growing into his glory. If he would only allow his best to shine through, to burst through, the world will be gifted in a tremendous way.

Thomas' father was absent throughout his childhood. Like most women, his loving mother, placed total blame on his father for being absent from the home. Perhaps there was hurtful things said that left Thomas with little respect for his father or black men in general. Those pains and hurt will last until we discover the truth. The truth is we can accept the past with all of its regrets and lessons and move on in LOVE.
We must be willing to release it totally!

Thomas, I Love You so much. Keep forgiving. Keep loving. You have a unique gift that is only yours to share with the world. The world is anxiously awaiting you!

Thank God for Teachers

Dr. C.C. Coleman

Pastor Coleman performed the ceremony for my marriage to Jeff Tyson in 1972. I have been blessed with more than thirty years of friendship with this wonderful man.

Pastor Coleman was Jeff's parents' minister at Ajalon Baptist Church in Compton. Mr. and Mrs. Tyson took responsibility for securing the minister because at the time I was not a member nor attending services anywhere. I don't remember much about our first meeting, other than Pastor Coleman performed the services.

In 1979, I was divorced and the proud owner of my first house, a home that I was buying by myself. My first major endeavor after the divorce.

There was a church at the corner of my block, only one house separated us. And as the Universal Spirit would ordain it, Pastor Coleman was the minister. He recognized me first, after all I was in denial about that marriage. So the minister that had performed the services had no place in my memory that did not bother Pastor Coleman.

One just has to meet Pastor Coleman to understand that he 'cannot' be forgotten! A strong spiritual presence and soul, tall, handsome, warm and consistently spoke his mind.

Pastor visited me and my son, Malcolm, regularly. I soon began to look forward to his taps on the front door calling out, "Tyson are you home?"

New Life Christian Church, the church on the corner, also provided an educational program. Malcolm started in Kindergarten and graduated from the sixth grade at New Life.

The learning experience my son received was the best possible beginning he could have received from any private school, exemplary of Pastor Coleman's standards. I remain thankful to Pastor Coleman and his incredible staff at New Life.

Each student was allowed to grow intellectually at their own ability, not held back due to pre-arranged time tables for learning. By the time Malcolm graduated from the sixth grade he was successfully and easily doing ninth grade work.

I became very active in the school and served as President of the Parent Teacher Fellowship for the majority of the years that Malcolm attended. I served in as many capacities as I could handle, to continue the excellent educational program that was being offered to the students. My experience was very fruitful. Pastor Coleman never hesitated to express his appreciation for the work I was accomplishing. Those were very good years. Pastor Coleman taught me the power of appreciation.

My relationship with Pastor Coleman has more than grown over these last twenty plus years. He and his wife, Jo, literally adopted me and Malcolm. I never called and he didn't answer. He stayed concerned about our welfare. I can still call on Pastor Coleman for encouragement, advice and prayer, and know he will be available to me. Pastor Coleman officiated at my beloved step-mother's funeral in 1989. He's been a friend to my entire family. We love him very much and that love is returned by him to us.

I now make my home in Atlanta, Georgia but I stay connected with Pastor Coleman who now lives in Huntsville Texas. I know and can always depend on him to support me, as I journey through life. My son and entire family knows that as well.

Pastor Coleman, I love you. You have contributed to my spiritual development in so many positive ways. I appreciate your tough love, your get in the face type of love.

Constantly sharing the love and truth of God with all who will listen. I consider you my father because you have always treated me with concern like a father. Words alone cannot demonstrate my gratitude so as my appreciation I allow my actions to demonstrate the life lessons I have learned from you. Always honor God. Be truthful.

Stand firm in your beliefs. Tell the story like it is - in other words don't pretty it up for the listener - or it could lose some of its meaning.

I hadn't spoken with Pastor Coleman in about four years and I was frantic trying to locate him. Visited his home in Lynwood California only to discover it had been sold.

Called the last number I had for him and it had been disconnected! I was so upset. As my absolute last resort I called information and got his number, Praise God. The area code had changed, the number was still the same. Our modern technology had created undue stress on me. The lesson I learned from this experience was never allow too much time to pass before contacting those Angels you've met along the way.

Mr. Zerl Presley

Zerl Presley is his name, being Spirit filled is his game! Mr. Presley was my music teacher in junior high school. My adopted dad in life. My Spiritual teacher. Mr. Presley is a jovial spirit, plump and vibrates with laughter.

His joy is infectious.

As band and orchestra leader he was serious in teaching and our learning. I can picture that worried - will they ever get it? - look on his face now. He would follow that facial expression with a look of pity and then hang his head down as he held on tightly to his stand! We were an excellent group of musicians by the end of the school year.
Or at least that's how I felt or chose to remember that experience until…..

30 (thirty) years later, while I was working as a sales counselor who walks into the store? Mr. Presley immediately began to tell 'his' side of the story. His tale was so interesting and full of good old fashioned joy that soon everyone in the store from the Manager to the customers were all gathered around him.

Mr. Presley described how awful I played, how he couldn't wait until I graduated so he wouldn't have to listen to my 'off' playing of the violin, of how I kept taking orchestra!

He was hilarious and I dared not attempt to quiet him. He told his now captive audience of how fat I was as a teenager. He told how extremely well my brother William played his horn and obviously that's where the musical talent in my family stopped. We were crying with laughter. He brightened the entire store and no one forgot that day and his story. He still had that same magnetism. He infected people with joy!

Mr. Presley also ministered to the youth. As a child I would sometimes accompany him to church. At the time I was contemplating my relocation to Atlanta was when Mr. Presley happened into the store where I was working.

It was all in Divine Time. As usual, Mr. Presley invited me and my sister, Janice, to join him the following Sunday. We graciously accepted. We attended services at two different locations. The first was the same church I had attended as a teenager. The second church, he was a scheduled speaker that day.

The Minister asked the congregation if anyone had a special prayer need. I advised of my need to be sure that the move I was making was the right one for me. The church prayed and I received my answer. There was no doubt from that day to this that my move was in Divine Order!

Mr. Presley thank you for your gift of joy and laughter. Thank you for allowing me to take your orchestra classes! Thank you for always being a kind and loving spirit.

I love You! Thank you for serving as a role model to so many teenagers!

Mr. George McKenna

Best known for his achievement at Washington High School in Los Angeles as depicted in the movie, **Lean On Me**.

As one of his students at Jordan High School in Watts, Mr. McKenna's influence was very powerful. Mr. McKenna is a very humble and inspiring individual. His style of teaching forced his students to achieve excellence in knowledge.

I was taught trigonometry and math analysis, two subjects I thought I would never master. I liked math and felt challenged by the subjects. Mr. McKenna made learning fun. Learning was non-threatening, you learned because you desired to learn not because you had to. Mr. McKenna has a gentle spirit, oh but I've seen his wrath when someone had the audacity to disrespect him that he just did not tolerate.

He is an honorable person. He constantly taught us by his actions and words - not to esteem him but our own personal intelligence. All he ever did was help bring out our genius, the best each student had to offer.

Mr. McKenna was always telling jokes, mainly to relax us. His nature was consumed with joy and he shared that without hesitation. Mr. McKenna, without a doubt, is a Master Educator and dynamic leader. He achieved his success by sincerely loving what he did. He loved young people. He loved watching us grow intellectually, he loved sharing his wisdom. Mr. McKenna thoroughly enjoyed all people. He is a powerful person, Dynamic personality.

In his last years working with the education system he became an administrator. By knowing Mr. McKenna's love of interaction with young people I can't imagine he was fulfilled in that position. He will never be an old person, always young and full of life. A staff position would slowly kill his spirit.

He still attends Jordan High School functions/reunions. He is still held in the highest of esteem by those that were blessed with his gift of teaching and friendship.

Mr. McKenna is a friend, never too busy or important to answer letters or phone calls. Mr. McKenna was personal, while teaching a whole class he coached each student individually to achieve excellence.

As we became adults he would tell us to call him George. He will always be Mr. McKenna to me. I love you George McKenna.

I still share in the same spirit I learned from you over twenty years ago. I help people to achieve their own excellence.

I teach from an attitude of humbleness and joy. Thank You for who you are. God has richly blessed the Universe with your presence. You have blessed God by allowing your goodness to be shared.

Dr. Robert Schmidt

A psychiatrist with Kaiser Permanente in California, my teacher and my friend. Dr. Schmidt is a well documented and very respected medical professional, an author and photographer. He and his wife love to travel around the world, experiencing all that life has to offer.

I first met Dr. Schmidt in the emergency room of Kaiser Hospital in 1984. I had driven myself there after experiencing severe chest pains. I was too frightened not to go and too scared to call for an ambulance. As each test result returned within a normal range, they referred me to the Mental Health Department, Dr. Schmidt was on duty that day.

Initially, I was upset because I felt they thought I was crazy! I had been in so much pain, hurt for such a long time that whatever they thought finally did not matter. I desperately wanted to be healed. Yet even though I knew I needed help, wanted badly for the aches and pains to vanish, I was not an easy patient.

I am so deeply grateful to Dr. Schmidt for his professionalism and dedication to assisting his patients with their treatment and complete recovery.

Yes, I freely and openly admit to spending years in therapy. Back then was a completely different scenario. My ego was so big yet so extremely fragile. The questions that kept repeating themselves in my head was 1) how can I tell my family and friends? And 2) my job needed me to be strong how can I tell them what happened? The voice, my inner voice was very strong. I was using the wrong language, the wrong tone. I had made myself invincible, a self proclaimed SUPERWOMAN, you know the kind, I can do it all and all by myself. That self destructive description had eaten away at my very soul. My body attacked itself – it yelled "STOP THIS NONSENSE – YOU NEED HELP GIRL!!" and off to the emergency room I went.

To help me manage the terrible mood swings Dr. Schmidt prescribed two medications, he gave full descriptions and instructions on the how and why to's. After several return visits, I believe I was going weekly or twice weekly, Dr. Schmidt was intrigued because there was no improvement with me.

He asked if I had gotten the prescription filled, I told him yes. After a few moments, still puzzled, he asked if I were taking the pills according to the directions. This was when Dr. Schmidt learned of my deep fear of becoming addicted to prescription medicine.

That entire session was spent in a very detailed explanation of my hormonal imbalance. That the medication was necessary to restore the natural balance AND I would not have to take the medicines any longer than absolutely necessary! Dr. Schmidt was so relieved when I finally agreed to try them for awhile.

Being stubborn was not aiding my well being. At times I would become so anxious, excited my blood pressure would be critically elevated. Dr. Schmidt would lead me in visualization techniques, played music of the sounds of nature. Although I was mostly open to recovery I was not always receptive to healing.

The more I learned to trust Dr. Schmidt and
his abilities, the less defensive I became.
He expended a lot of energy to crack my
shell, to get to the root cause.

As my healing became evident Dr. Schmidt
directed the following sessions on
prevention. Our discussions became more in
depth about my childhood and other
experiences.

One day Dr. Schmidt, feeling confident with
our relationship, asked me 'Why do talented,
capable women subject themselves to and
tolerate less than desirable
traits/behaviors in men?' He was perplexed
because he said the problem was a recurring
one with several of his female patients.
That began a dialog between us that has
lasted for years. We share information such
as books that deal with the subject.

As I let my defensive guard down and became
vulnerable and open to sharing and learning
Dr. Schmidt and I became good friends. When
my healing was complete, our roles reversed.
Dr. Schmidt would share openly with me about
issues he was facing. We continue to share
with each other.

Whenever I visit Los Angeles I go by to
visit him. On one visit I was told by the
receptionist that I could not see him
because I was no longer a member of Kaiser.
Dr. Schmidt told me if I ever encounter a
problem just to tell the receptionist I'm
his friend! And I know and accept that
completely.

Dr. Schmidt thank you for not giving up on
me. I know I was a difficult patient. Thank
you for caring enough to stand toe to toe

with me as I reluctantly removed each of the masks I used to shield myself from pain. Thank you for wanting only the best for me. Thank you for helping me discover the truth of who I am. Thank you for your friendship, love, admiration and support.

Dr. Schmidt treated me with more than just pills and counseling sessions, He added the truth of God! Thanks God for using Dr. Robert Schmidt to help me mend my brokenness. I Love You, Dr. Schmidt.

Raymond Rasberry

Mr. Rasberry was the esteemed Choir Director at Disciples of Christ Church in Lynwood California where I was a member.

When I finally agreed to join the choir this wonderful soul asked me to sing soprano. I couldn't stop laughing, you see I possess a very deep bass-sounding voice. That's my definition anyway. Mr. Rasberry assured me I could develop my voice to sing soprano. I thought to myself if he thinks I can, I'll give it a try. Although I said okay I did not truly believe it was possible.

As Scripture reminds us "You can do ALL things through Christ who strengthens you". The time came for me to display my talents, to sing the much anticipated soprano lead of a song that Mr. Rasberry had written. I must admit I did an incredible job during that performance.

Mr. Rasberry I thank you for teaching me how to sing, how to stretch my abilities, most importantly to have faith.

Rev. Ricardo Rivers

Rev. Ric was my first teacher at Hillside. The class 'Lessons In Truth' was an awesome learning experience. I discovered the meaning of my name and heard for the first time a very beautiful and sentimental account of why the name La Sandra was bestowed upon me. That was the first class in a series of learning I have participated in at Hillside Chapel and Truth Center.

Rev. Ric is a very warm and inviting young soul. Rev. Ric was so well grounded in TRUTH principles one would not have known he was a senior in the Barbara King School of Ministry but a veteran Minister. This young brother eluded a very spiritual presence.

Rev. Ric became a friend in helping his students discover the Truth of their being. There was so much to release, to allow room for a more divine acceptance of ourselves. His intuition served him well in realizing what we needed.

He helped me build the foundation of my transitional stage of life. Like a Master Teacher he was careful not to lecture rather he facilitated this evolvement. He taught me I know that I know was the arrival point, to believe a thing or think something is not fully accepting it. When words could not explain and you didn't force a verbal description – that was the exact moment when it became REAL, at the deepest level possible, the spiritual level.

It took some time before I could honestly say 'I know that I know' during the development stages of growth. I longed for that deep state of complete trust that Rev. Ric displayed repeatedly. He was a true source of inspiration.

I often called on Rev. Ric for guidance and support in my early stages. When my nephew was savagely beaten Rev. Ric was the Spiritual comforter for me and my son.

Involved in another project when I arrived at Hillside, he suspended all other activity until he had prayed and comforted me through his counseling.

To be in attendance at his ordination service was extremely special for me. I cried tears of joy for I knew Rev. Ric was submitting wholeheartedly to his highest calling. I am very proud to know this marvelous soul. Very excited that my life has been touched in such a powerful way by him.

Rev. Ric, I Love You. I bless you, I appreciate you and I thank God for YOU.

Pastor Carl Booker

I first met Pastor Booker at a meeting neither of us actually wanted to attend. Although we attended out of obligation, we have concluded that God brought us together for a divine purpose.

For two months we were close constant companions. Developing a strong bond. I witnessed his personal dedication and commitment to teaching everyone, especially people facing extreme challenges in their lives.

Pastor Booker is an extremely warm, caring, soft spoken, dynamic man. I was immediately drawn to his presence.

My introduction to Spiritual healing through an oral presentation was by an invitation Pastor Booker extended to me. Speaking before an audience was not new to me but this occasion was my initial experience at being the featured Spiritual speaker.

I was so excited. I never anticipated the rewards I would be blessed with. I had mingled with the ladies at My Sisters House before the program started. I decided beforehand that I would not prepare a speech but would allow Spirit to guide and direct me. It was the most exhilarating experience I had ever encountered.

I had commentated numerous fashion shows and facilitated training classes for hundreds. But this was so absolutely different. As I stood before these women that I had just spoken with, we became one entity. The Spirit in me swelled and filled me with so much compassion and love for these women who were temporarily housed at this shelter.

As I looked into the eyes of these very beautiful women, I saw me! We became one body. The women needed a love treatment, unconditional love for themselves.

I am so indebted to Pastor Booker for providing me this opportunity which prompted me to build an entire program whose sole purpose is to heal, recognizing the wounds people may have that leads to abusive situations.

This book is a direct outcome of the urging I received to bless others with the type of healing only I could provide.

Pastor Booker, I Love You. I thank you for being such a strong Christian, filled with love for everyone you come in contact with. You have truly been and inspiration and motivation in my life. I thank you for allowing God to use you in such a powerful way!!

Bosom Buddies

I have deliberated on the title for this
chapter.
These men have been especially close to me,
have had a
major positive impact on my life.
So I am adding a chapter just for them,
My Bosom Buddies!

Tip

Nathaniel Tyler, Tip is my adopted big brother but he has been more than that to me. So I include him here to honor the powerful friendship we have had over the many years.

Nathaniel was tagged with the nickname TIP because of his running style on the gridiron – the football field. Yes, he ran on his toes!

As children, teenagers and young adults Tip was consistently there for me. He helped me through much of my life stages and Challenges. Tip was very instrumental in my personal growth and development. We shared on such a very deep, personal level. Tip was my strength as a teenager. He would probably say it isn't so because he is a modest individual.

Just as Tip is a valuable part of my family, he is the godfather of my niece Juandessa. I have been included with his family as well.

His brother Terry and I attended high school at the same time. I, we know each other's family very well. Tip's daughter Nate is like my daughter. I had not realized just how close we had been until his mother died last year. I attended the funeral, although I was not close to his parents, I felt the pain experienced by those mourning.

Nathaniel's parents had been married for over fifty years! I saw the emptiness in his father's eyes. So sad. I had a difficult time even visualizing two people being together, happily for more years than I had been alive. That is still an awesome

Accomplishment to me. My sincere appreciation to the Tyler's for allowing me to share their son during my life.

Tip we shared a wonderful friendship. I appreciate all the wonderful acts of kindness you expressed to me. The actions are too many to name. I know you can remember all the crazy times. I love you and bless you and your family. I appreciate the bond we have shared together.

H.D. Holt

Henry Darnell Holt - it took years for me to discover what H.D. stood for. That's the kind of person this man is, always keeping something from you, from me anyway!

My relationship with H.D. ran the gamut from business associate, employer, close friend and brother.

Regardless of the position we found ourselves in, deep philosophical discussions were forever a huge component.

I don't remember how I first met H.D., he would probably blame it on my senility! I do remember our first business venture. He was commissioned to do some embroidery work on our staff jackets for Ubitquitdus Modeling Company. H.D. primarily did silk screening.

He had a nice business facility. His work was consistently of high quality, so H.D. got repeat business from Ubitquitdus. Our friendship developed as a result of the many business deals we completed.

We would meet for business discussions; how to structure, when to expand, attract the right people into our businesses? These questions would lead into hours of conversation.

When I opened Nu Vision Modeling and Entertainment, H.D. became my official printer for all of our company's apparel. H.D. taught me how to silk screen, although he constantly complained of my slow speed.

He appreciated me helping him during his busy periods. H.D. is very creative. He has designed and modified original Juneteenth shirts for the past twelve years. H.D. actually designed most of the caps, aprons, jackets and so on using his own creative genius. He is very talented and has a keen sense of business.

H.D. and I went into partnership and began creating flyers and business brochures. We were forever creating additional opportunities for ourselves.

I was more impressed with his cooking skills. He could fry some fish! The best tasting fish you have ever eaten. Melts in your mouth kind of good.

We developed a business plan and sought financing for his eatery. H.D. experienced many delays and setbacks. That did not stop him. H.D. would set up his fish fry equipment at all community events in Los Angeles and nearby communities.

Always selling out very quickly. I would beg him to fry fish all the time. It became a weekly treat. I didn't mind working with him, he fed me real good!

We were very close, our families knew of each other well. As a matter of fact, H.D. continues to visit my father as often as he can. And brings him fish on Fridays!

H.D. has been married to Renita for approximately twenty eight years. They have two wonderful grown sons.

My brother was having problems in his marriage, he finally shared with me. H.D. had denied Renita a place in the marriage and home. H.D. did everything; worked his business; took the boys to school, sometimes different schools and to any appointments they have had; picked them up from school; shopped for groceries and cooked all the meals; washed the clothes and cleaned the house.

He refused to hear me the first twenty times I said it, he didn't allow Renita an opportunity to contribute to the household. He was forcing her out of the marriage. H.D. can be extremely difficult to talk to, especially when he thinks he has the correct answer. Oh the conversations around my conclusion!

I must be crazy, she should appreciate everything he does for her. He was just helping out. When H.D. finally conceded he found his marriage began to improve rapidly. It was a long battle but one I had to fight, he was my friend. Renita is a beautiful woman and loves my brother unconditionally. She now enjoys her home and family.

H.D. graduated from college in 2001. I surprised him by showing up as my father's date at the Graduation Dinner.

He was so excited, we started our usual confrontations at the table, everyone laughed because that was our normal communication style. I am so very Proud of H.D. for completing one of his primary goals in life.

I don't care what they say about you H.D., I knew you could do it ...ONE DAY!
I love you.

This letter was received after the writing began.
Gotta Love ya H.D.

Dear Sandy,

Thank you for including me in your book. I have for a long time thought that you had a lot of positive things to
say that other people, men and women, could benefit from. I know that by exchanging ideas with you I have been enlightened in my own relationship. I hope that I have been a source of enlightenment for you as well.

First, I think that we as black men have to stop thinking of any outside influence as reason fro stopping us from reaching our goals. We are in charge of our own destiny to a much larger degree than we sometimes admit to.

We don't always reach our goals and get everything we want, but we could achieve even more if we complain less and try harder. That is not to say that there are not outside forces that are aimed at stopping us from achieving more, but we have to stay focused. Those things that are used against us to stop us from going forward that we can fight I say we should fight. Those things that only take up our time and serve to piss us off, we should not ignore but we should make note of them and not let them stop us from achieving our individual goals.

It reminds me of a story told to me about a little boy who was playing baseball with his friends in a field one day. The little boy brought his dog with him while he played. The boy knew that his dog would always get involved when he played with others and would interfere and mess up the game. So the boy brought a rope to tie the dog to a tree.

But in his hast to tie the rope he missed the knot in the rope and the dog was not tied at all. After the game, the boy, upon seeing that the rope was not tied thought that the dog was doing the right thing, but instead the dog did not know that he was not tied and stayed in place. The story to me is it says that some of us have been mentally tied for so long we no longer test the rope.

Secondly, I think that getting older is an advantage that our society looks upon as a curse. As I get older I feel more aware of everything around me and I appreciate everything more. The things one learns from getting older can only be passed on by the passing of time. Experience can be relayed in word but it cannot be relayed to another one's experience. Each person, even if they experience the same thing, may come away with a different impression from that same experience.

Anyway I talk too much. May your book be as positive an experience on the literary world as you have been on me.

Any grammatical mistakes were intentional if you don't find none dat was intentional also.

Your friend The Great one H.D. Holt

Hollywood

Here's a big shout out to my biggest fan – Rafiyal Saxxton Tezdale Hollywood III.

This most creative designer, Mr. Hollywood, was best known for his Cherry Pink Designs.

Hollywood has an enormous heart! Some folks criticized him because he was extremely overweight. I say was because I haven't seen Hollywood for a long time. He had difficulty with walking because of his weight. However, his weight could not and did not block his creative ability.

And he simply adored Beautiful Women! His designs were always flattering to the soft feminine silhouette, strictly sensuous.

Hollywood encouraged all designers, cheered each as they displayed their designs. A team leader!

Hollywood was very protective of me. Would boldly tell people 'Don't mess with Sandy, that's my girl!' It was not said in a romantic manner but a friendly and assertive tone. Hollywood would visit Nu Vision often. Dropping by to just say hello and offer words of support. And also to see if I needed protection.

Hollywood I Love You. I pray you are still designing those fantastic outfits for the beautiful women of the world. YOU GOT SKILL!!!!

Mc Ray Pettigrew

McRay observed me closely for more than two years as I learned all the intricate details of running a 12-step recovery facility.

In the end he told me, "Sandy you cannot save a person unless they recognize they need the help". McRay knew I was getting deeply involved with the hopes of saving a very dear relative in their recovery from alcoholism. I did not want to hear those words. I knew McRay was absolutely correct, yet there was this pain in me for my relative.

Wanted to see them recover so badly I thought I could show them the way and they would automatically follow. I worked diligently at learning and performing duties to be able to open my own recovery home.

The one problem I had with the 12-step program was each person would stand and introduce themselves and add "I'm an alcoholic!"

I thought for a long time before I finally asked this question of McRay but I couldn't hold it in any longer. I said, "When is a person no longer an alcoholic?" Some had been attending meetings for over twenty years. I felt they were now sober individuals.

I believe the program is incredible, hundreds of thousands of lives have been saved by AA, I just wanted them not to be required to label themselves as alcoholics.

I met some wonderful people attending the meetings and shared deeply with many of the residents at the recovery homes. Each one a tremendous soul that just looked for their salvation and validation in the wrong spot!

A genuine loving friendship developed between McRay and I. I remained an active part of his program 'Bridge for the Needy' and the founding of his program 'Last House on the Block'.

McRay became an integral part of Nu Vision, co-chairing the men's group - For Men Only. We supported each other as much as we possibly could. Nu Vision performed a tribute fundraiser show for the now late O.C. Smith which featured The Coasters.

The majority of the models did not know either of these legendary greats. The show served as a lesson in musical history for them.

Everyone benefited.

McRay, I appreciate you, your tireless dedication to serving others through your recovery programs. I love the precious times of sharing we experienced together. I am grateful for your candidness with me.
I Love You - - Mc Ray Pettigrew

Dave Jackson

D.J., my buddy from the Motor City of Detroit.

Dave was forever tickling me, making me laugh.

When I would get too deeply involved with performing my job duties, Dave would sneak up from behind me and tickle me, like one does a little child being playful. Dave would always caution me to take it easy.

It upset him when I was working so much overtime. I had taken on a job that had been neglected and therefore seriously backlogged. Dave said it often, "Sandy you can't get it all done in one day!"

Barely taking a lunch or break, I was determined to succeed.

Dave proved to be right! He had seen people come in, tackle the job dutifully, only to get completely burned out. As my friend he warned me against becoming a casualty. Dave, I know it seemed I didn't listen until burnout creeped up on me. I was listening and I sincerely appreciate your genuine concern.

When I transferred to another station, Dave was assigned to spear head a major change taking place within the company. Dave would visit me at my new site to train me and the station personnel, providing additional support.

The system had many initial flaws, which most new programs have. Dave and I worked as a team in identifying system problems to ensure a smooth operation of the new system. This was always done on his time off, which was extremely meaningful to me.

When Dave decided to become an Independent Contractor, I helped him with his business plan by providing resources and personal knowledge. Due to his high work ethics, his company was exceeding the targets set and surpassed the majority of established Independent Contractors. Dave consistently takes pride in each of his undertakings.

Thanks for watching over me and being concerned with my wellness.

I Love You, Dave.

Wakaho

My African brother from Kenya, Africa.

Our friendship blossomed in large part because I wanted to honor him by learning and calling him by his birth name, and not the American name Bill he had adopted. I wanted to know about his homeland, as much as he could tell me.

When I moved from one home to another, Wakaho graciously offered his services and his twenty four foot truck to get it done. We completed the move in one trip!

As a Supervisor facing unseen problems with freight being picked up or delivered I often sought Wakaho's help.

He remained dependable throughout our working relationship. Wakaho tired of the city life and moved his family back to Kenya.

He wanted his children to experience the freedom of life Africa offered. When he described the countryside he was vivid in his colorful recollections of a picturesque place; Animals roaming free in the wilderness.

Like a big Zoo is how Wakaho described it. Wakaho and family are adjusting quite well. He is having a home built and has invited me to come for a visit when its completed.

Thanks Wakaho for teaching me about your homeland. Thanks for the magnificent authentic African sculptures you presented me before you left America.

See you in Kenya soon. I love you.

Arnold Scott

I met Arnold shortly after my last adopted son had become seriously involved with his soul mate. However I am choosing not to call him a son, so far he has been more like a brother, a very special friend.

Arnold and I met at Hillside Chapel and Truth Center, where we are both members. We are both a part of the Volunteer Ministry's Core Team. The Core Team was charted with the responsibility of building the Volunteer Ministry.

We had spent one Thursday morning together observing a food pantry operation at a local church. We were busy learning there was little time for us to become acquainted. The following day we worked side by side stuffing our church bulletins.

This time I told Arnold about my pattern with adopted sons after he had very openly shared some delicate personal concerns with me. I said 'Okay God let's go to work!' and I started smiling.

Since our meeting, which has only been a few months, we have become very close friends. Being supportive, being encouraging and sharing Blessings and lessons. Arnold's positive energy is extremely powerful and infectious. We are learning almost daily of the similarities we share. I really enjoy Arnold and his bold spirit.

Arnold is a dynamic soul. At one of our Volunteer meetings he shared with us a treat he had for his parents. He was so proud as he shared complete outfits he had purchased for his parents to wear to the college graduation of his eldest brother, who was receiving his Doctorate degree.

Not only did he buy the outer garments but also he bought belts, ties, stockings, shoes, underwear and jewelry! We all felt so impressed by his generosity towards his parents. Arnold is a unique person, so deliberately excited about life and all its wonder.

We attended a Salsa dance class sponsored by the Singles Ministry at Hillside. We had so much fun. Neither had disclosed what excellent dancers both of us are. We just went to support the ministry and to have fun. In no time at all, Arnold had become the instructor for the men! He is so smooth on the dance floor, undeniably enjoying himself . So I look forward to finding what else we will share in the future.

Our newest project is developing a training workshop for the leaders of our church. We are also developing a new enterprise since both of our backgrounds are founded in training. I know we will make a superb team. Look out world here we come!

Arnold - I Love You, I Bless You and I Appreciate You.

Willie Hood

When I met Mr. Hood he was in charge of the dock operations but not a Supervisor. When the opportunity came I recommended him highly for the promotion. Willie ran the show even before he had been given the responsibility.

Willie was experiencing problems with his adult son. Their relationship was strained because Willie was not present during his son's life. His son, not knowing how to explain the pain and anger he felt, lashed out at Willie. First verbally then physically.

Willie and I would discuss the challenges he was faced with. His initial response was to ignore the problem. Willie felt since he had not been available before why should he cause a problem now. We talked about the relationship for months. Realizing his son was reaching out for him, Willie accepted the responsibility of being a father to his son.

They are working on establishing a friendship now. The problems are disappearing as communication take hold of the situation. I am pleased that Willie stepped up to the plate instead of walking away.

Willie, Mr. Hood you are a good man and my good friend.
I Love You.

Peter Laing

My Jamaican brother who loves to play tricks on me.

An extremely loving and unselfish man. A nurturer and helper to everyone.

The most memorable characteristic of Peter was his fear of loving someone. When Peter met Tracey he fell in love instantly. He couldn't admit it to himself. As I listened to him the words described a cherished relationship, his eyes sparkled with delight and he blushed!

I didn't know Tracey at the time, I thought she was indeed one of the blessed women of the world to have a man, this man love her so completely. Because of Peter's preferred state of perfection he feared not being able to totally satisfy this rare gem. So the engagement was pending.

Peter talked with his coworkers, all of which were women, until he felt secure with himself. It was a long process. Peter, You know I love you!!

Their wedding reception was one of the most joyous celebrations I have ever witnessed.

So much love shared by each and every family member and guest. Little boys admiring their mothers as they danced with them. Friends truly honoring each other with JOY. Folks having unadulterated Fun.

No pretense or 'I'm too cute to act natural. Jamaican tradition was easily mixed in with the events of their day.

Peter still calls and disguises his voice. If I am not looking at my caller ID he fools me every single time.

I love our friendship. We have lifted each other up, Peter, I Love You. You are truly a very unique man.

Work Comrades

Working with the same company for twenty
three years, undoubtedly there were numerous
men who impacted me and my career I mention
here the ones that truly left their
trademark in my life and heart.

Mike Bell

My very first close work-related male friend happened to be Caucasian, a white man. Neither race nor color had an affect on our relationship, we were very dear friends.

Mike was my Manager from somewhere during the middle 'til the end of my twenty three year career with Pacific Bell Telephone Co. in California.

Mike believed in my abilities, he trusted me which provided me numerous opportunities. If I indicated I wanted to do something, he opened the door for me. All I had to do was be prepared to walk through the door. I did that often, always thankful for the opportunity to grow in all areas.

Mike is a good person, always honest with me, in personal and professional concerns. Mike and I respected each other totally. I have shared time with his son Jamie and then fiancée, Lorraine.

Mike proudly attended my second wedding. I remember a couple of weeks before the ceremony Mike and I went out to lunch to discuss my future plans. Mike could be so naive about life!

He asked very pointed unexpected questions about if I would change my name, how my son was accepting the upcoming changes and he ended the conversation with a stern, serious face saying "You can always change your mind. If you have any doubt, promise me you will be true to yourself."

I know Mike held only my best in his heart.

Mike was a very meticulous dresser. Never a wrinkle in his clothes, hair always neat and in place, the kind of dresser one only saw in the magazines. I loved how he dressed and carried himself, so professional.

During one of our weekly Supervisor meetings, I was disturbed because Mike's hair was not in place. When we took a break, I went up to Mike and patted his hair into place. It just did not look right to me and I couldn't stand to see it messed up. So I did what any friend would do.

Later that afternoon, each of my fellow co-workers harassed me about playing in Mike's hair piece. I was stunned. I had no idea he wore a toupee. Talk about being naive, this time it was me.

Although each supervisor called and confirmed their belief about Mike's hair I refused to believe it. Not that there was anything wrong with a man wearing a hair piece, it looked very natural to me. So I bluntly asked Mike and he shared with me a story about an illness that had left him partially bald and he chose to wear the toupee.

I defended Mike to my fellow co-workers. They finally just agreed, Sandy doesn't think it's funny.

Mike loves soul food. Every chance he got to eat at a soul food restaurant he would be there. Harold and Belle's in Los Angeles became 'the' choice of eateries to celebrate all occasions. The food there is excellent; the cook was from New Orleans.

Even after my retirement I would continue to visit Mike or socialize with him.

I haven't seen Mike in a long time. My love, appreciation and respect remain intact. I grew to my limits not the corporation limits, based on my title. I traveled throughout the state training, developing new programs and whatever else I would volunteer to lead all with Mike's blessings.

Once I teased Mike, told him I wanted his job. He asked if I were serious and when I said yes he took vacation. It was very challenging. I gained a great deal more respect for Mike's position. I was extremely happy when he returned.

All went well, but I never made that statement again. Of the programs I initiated and had control over, my accomplishments were rewarded handsomely by the Company; plaques, accolades, special events with awards.

Mike, wherever you may be please know I Love You and our friendship remains a very important, positive segment in my life!

Larry High

Larry had not been working in our office very long before he would become my guardian angel.

I was perfecting my management knowledge, taking home volumes of the Company's tariffs, SOP standard operating procedure, studying nightly.

I was a single mother and had recently purchased my first home that was being remodeled at the time. Completely Stressed.

One day I started feeling ill and felt against my better judgment, I should go home. I entered Larry's office to tell him I was leaving, would he please take care of my group for me.

Larry would not allow me to leave. I insisted I just needed to go home. Larry forced me to sit down, asked for my mother's phone number and called her immediately. He kept talking calmly to me.

I was getting irritated, please Larry I just need to go home. When the ambulance arrived I was looking around to see who the paramedics had come to take to the hospital. To my complete surprise - they were there for ME! I was having heart palpitations and elevated blood pressure.

Being fully recuperated, Larry had a big brother talk with me. He had been a medic in the military. He told me my finger nails were blue and he feared for my life. He had seen situations like that before and not all the individuals survived!

I Love You Larry High. I thank God for you. I thank you for being my Guardian angel back in May 1980.

May God bless you always and forever.

John Lamascus

John was the kindest, most gentle spirit I ever worked with. Because of his style of managing his Supervisors, our results were

always the best in the state. John always
backed his Supervisors and gave us
flexibility to perform our jobs.

John was a Christian and he proudly shared
his love of God with all, employees and
customers. I learned how to remain in the
right mental awareness in dealing fairly
with people.

You may not always get rewarded here on
earth, just knowing you did the right thing
was sufficient reward. That was a powerful
lesson to learn especially during a time
when downsizing was just becoming the
popular thing to do for large corporations.

John was released from Pacific Bell, even
though our group ranked #1 consistently,
repeatedly.

Dick Little

Mr. Little was our District Manager, the
most humane higher level manager in my
career. Mr. Little sincerely loved all
people.

It was his habits of greeting everyone with
a BIG bear hug that I included that element
in my management style. Mr. Little would buy
his entire organization books and tokens. I
still have my copy of "Hug Therapy" and my
hug coupons!

Ed Dragon

Ed was never a calm individual. We could be
in the middle of a serious discussion and he
would just get up, pick up his briefcase,
turn off the lights and leave. I would still

be sitting there, in the dark, wondering when the conversation ended. He did this often, it became routine.

I learned to stay focused and centered!!

This next Business comrade is a man I worked with for years learning a completely new industry.

When he found out I was writing a book, he insisted his comments be included.

April 23, 2002

As the Executive Director of UBITQUITDUS (a youth based personal development program) of Los Angeles, Sandy Rodgers was an active and dedicated staff member.
One of her roles was designing clothes for the nearly 100 models of the organization.

She joined the company in 1985 and was instrumental in building the Largest Minority-Owned Modeling/charm School in Southern California. Her major priority was aiding in the growth and self-awareness of the school. People ages two through adults.

In 1991, Rodgers opened her own Entertainment (Nu Vision Modeling) and continued to help inspire youth. As a talented and successful businesswoman, Sandy Rodgers motivated numerous inner-city children to become confident and goal oriented.

Some of the most prominent community groups and individuals to work with Ms. Rodgers included: Los Angeles Mayors Tom Bradley and Richard Riordan, Muhammad Ali, State Senator

Diane Watson, California (Democratic) Congresswoman Maxine Waters, Council Member Mark Ridley-Thomas and recognized by California Governor Pete Wilson. Ms. Rodgers is a recipient of the Outstanding Young Women in America award of 1988.

Fabian Brown

An educator, creative genius, excellent choreographer, brilliant in the modeling industry.

As with everything I allowed my son to participate in, I became very active with UBITQUITDUS Modeling. I surveyed the company, attended a few of the shows and had several meetings with Mr. Brown prior to enrolling Malcolm into the program at UBITQUITDUS.

I was immediately impressed with the professionalism of the models, particularly the children. The precision of the Tiny Tots was incredible, small children modeling on que with precision. The staff was well trained and knowledgeable about the Company's history and mission.

I began as a parent, became the staff Designer and subsequently took on the responsibility as the Assistant Director. I was instrumental in building a phenomenal Parent Group. In the former position I had tremendous responsibility in the daily operation of UBITQUITDUS.

By the time the enrollment had increased we were performing more often, at every major Hotel and convention centers in Southern California.

Fabian's influence on the models was immense. Mr. Brown would teach class, developed routines and rehearsed the models until everything was perfected. Success was imminent. UBITQUITDUS's models were touring with Ebony Fashion Fair, several of the models performed yearly with the famed Bronner Brothers Hair Show in Atlanta, several models have achieved fame as Television actors. All models had higher self-esteem.

The Parent Group was outstanding. Each volunteering their time willfully for the success of the company. We were organized, professional and uniformly dressed. We built the company into a magnificent power house.

Mr. Brown had great alliances with prominent businessmen such as Jon Linscott of Black Gold Magazine and Jaime Berger of Clarasol Productions to name a few.

When people witnessed the company they were moved to contribute in whatever way they could.

This all took place in a rather short period of time. Fabian hadn't prepared himself for the huge success his company had become. I think he was consumed with fear, fear of success maybe even failure. Fabian stopped doing the very things that had built the company initially. He took his eyes off the prize - the children.

Egos grew larger than the company itself. The company began to disintegrate. People started leaving. Fabian's health began to decline. I had always admired Fabian and his creative ability. I did not know how to help him. I eventually left the company also.

Thank you Fabian Brown for allowing me so many opportunities to learn and grow in the Modeling industry.

Thank you for supporting my designs by showcasing them at the Beverly Center, International Gold and all the shows.
Thank you for helping me to become a well documented Designer by the many featured articles done on LaTyson Designs.

More importantly thank you for educating all the children that had the privilege of participating with UBITQUITDUS MODELING COMPANY. Trust me your genius will never be forgotten. Just ask any of your former students!!!

Circuit City - Atlanta Home Delivery

June 1995 I arrived in Atlanta Georgia; ready and willing for a new start in my new beautiful homeland.

New beginnings can be frightening, especially when every little thing is NEW. I entered into a job in a warehouse filled with absolutely wonderful men! I had never worked in anything remotely similar to a warehouse.

There were so many, I'm sure some names will be omitted but here goes - Big Al, Marcus Sherman, Lawrence, Rich, Scott Lynch, Trooper, Tony, Mike, Ricky, Jesse, Robert, Efrem, Carlos, J.R., Kenny, Jacob, Mitch, Arn, Mackey, Gary and Paul. The guys were all marvels.

This group of men served as my first family in Atlanta. They loved me and took care of me, protecting and shielding me from all hurt and harm. Some served as father figures - Big Al and Robert Jones (although younger than me).

Some were my big brothers - Marcus Sherman, Tony, Mike, Scott Lynch, Carlos Gonzales, and J.R. Some were best friends - Ricky, Efrem, Jesse and Paul. They were all my family, more importantly they were all my friends. And I thank God for each one of them.

Paul Tisdale

Paul became my very first friend after my move to Atlanta. He trusted me from the very beginning without really knowing me or who I was. At the time he needed a friend more than I did.

His entire life centered around Circuit City, thus all of his friends were also his co-workers. Paul was carrying a heavy burden that he had to share, something so life altering he deeply desired to share his pain with a friend. A friend who would not repeat his story.

I showed up in Divine time to help Paul. He was separated from his wife and children. Hurting so badly I wondered how he functioned on a daily basis. He was searching for answers to resolutions between him and his wife. But who could he turn to was the question that plagued him every minute of the day.

Paul lived only a few blocks from me. Although we did not visit each other we talked on the telephone for countless hours. We discussed his perception of his marriage and the challenges he was facing. I say it that way because ultimately it is 'our' perception of situations that create our reality. One person's perception may not be the other person's reality.

During our discussions we would tend to become so open that it caused disagreements. Neither of us was prepared to hear the brutal truth about ourselves. We fussed like married folk. Perhaps he missed that part of marriage, smile. We became joined at the hip and we toughed it out by using love and compassion as the foundation.

It was not always easy nor was it telling the other person what was wrong with them. We sought goodness in each other and at times literally yanked it out from its cleverly disguised place.

Upon reconciliation Paul's wife earnestly thanked me for investing time with her husband, which surely impacted the entire family.

Paul wherever you are and whatever you may be facing - accept my love for you is unconditional and sincere.

I LOVE YOU - - L.A.

Efrem McGruder

My running partner who was young in age yet old in wisdom.

Efrem and I spent time together not just partying throughout Atlanta metro area but we also developed the rebirth of Nu Vision.

Although I've lost contact with Efrem, he will forever be an exceptional segment of my life.

We had many discussions about love and life, dreams, goals, and the future. He was consistently steady on his course. Always setting realistic and attainable goals, looking forward with joy and faith. He reminded me of a rock, solid and firm.

Could be tossed or thrown yet did not lose his shape (his spirit). Efrem was determined to advance, slowly if necessary, in reaching his goals.

Efrem called me 'Shorty', I stand 5'1". We had a pool table in our employee lounge. Often there were pool tournaments. We shot pool daily. Although I don't call myself a pro, I play very well.

I won a lot of games, making shots that would amaze even myself. At those times Efrem affectionately called me 'Shorty Pimp'. Most of the men thought I couldn't play pool they would challenge me to a game.

Efrem would lean back and grin. As I won, he simply laughed at the men who had challenged me. We had fun.

Efrem continuously watched over me. Needed to make sure I was okay. He served as my shield. Most of his friends knew of me and our relationship. We were special to each other.

We would go the clubs and dance all night long, both sweating and hearts racing. Having so much fun nothing else mattered. We were close friends, business seekers, life students and assisted each other with discovering the best we had to offer. Ours was just an absolutely marvelous relationship.

We just drifted away from each other. I know Efrem is somewhere doing great things. Efrem possess a deep rooted spiritual background. He has faith in God, the creator of all things.

Always trust his prayers to be answered. I learned simply how to live in a slower paced environment with Efrem. He was never in a hurry about anything. Just relaxed and accepting life as it came to him.
Thanks Efrem for everything! I Love You!

Robert Jones

Robert was my Supervisor at Circuit City. He is a very large man, over six feet tall and a former wrestling champion. He was massive!

Robert earned everyone's respect because he first gave respect to everyone, when he came to Home Delivery.

He had earned a double Master's degree but was so incredibly down to earth. Would joke and tease, showered all the workers with praise. His style of management was not easily accepted by the higher levels of management.

Robert attempted to change, to be more demeaning, that just was not him. Thank God. He decided to be true to himself and deal with the consequences he was sure to encounter. Everyone, all of his employees, fully supported him and did everything we could to ensure his victory! And we succeeded. Good prevailed.

Robert is young and full of greatness. He has since left Circuit City and had worked for another company.

Today I am not sure where he is employed and what he is doing, I do know for sure that if Robert remains true to himself the sheer greatness within him will be released for the benefit of the entire planet.

Atlanta Committee for the Olympic Games (ACOG)

Working with ACOG in 1996 was heavily influenced by my good friend Gerald Henderson.

Gerald and I had worked together at Circuit City prior to him receiving a position with ACOG. When an opening became available for a Security Trainer, Gerald gave me a recommendation to Dick Weber, Security Training Manager.

I was subsequently blessed to be a Security Trainer working with GBI (Georgia Bureau of Investigation), Police and military personnel, and volunteers from all walks of life. This was such an incredible opportunity. My assignment was ninety miles from home in the picturesque city of Athens, Georgia.

I was immensely rewarded by working with the best team ACOG offered. This magnificent team was lead by Jerry Stoddard. Jerry is an Athens native and worked for the Athletics department at UGA. Jerry is such a warm, inviting soul. It was indeed my privilege to work with this man who showed sincere respect for everyone. Jerry's warmth and personality made the long, extensive days pass by quickly.

His responsibilities were widespread and completed with perfection.

Jerry, Ben and I ran the venues at Athens. We were an awesome team, each complimenting the other. We got the job done with professionalism and diplomacy, respect and concern and perhaps the most important was our love of all people.

The experience of working as a Security Trainer with the 1996 Olympics is an unrepeatable blessing. To Jerry,
Ben, William (Bill) A. Thomas and all the others who gave unselfishly…..I Salute You for a job well done.

Airborne Express

Airborne has been an exceptional experience for me.
I have become friends with and know some incredible men there. I have worked at the majority of stations in Atlanta. I
promise some names will be omitted not intentionally just there are so many wonderful men to honor.

Marv Tabor, Mike Martin, Greg Dial, John Rowan, Pat McDowell, Mike Drew, Mike Love, Les Wells, Jan Boling, Dwight Martin, Robert Toomer, Will, Phil, Jim, Neto, Carl, Calvin, Willie, Sunny, Leonard, Tyrone, Jimmy, Andrew, Carlos, Byron, Myron, Dave J., Mickey, T.J., Dave Fairbanks, Mike, Que, Stephone, Tony, Fred, Terrance, Dadriel, Will, Maurice, Wes, Jason, Peter, Tinsley,

Brad, Johnny, Chip, Jeff, Justin, John, Mike, Randolph, Tracy, Brian, Charles, Cecil, Dwayne, Ed, Saul, Julio and the list goes on.

My first day at Airborne Express in downtown Atlanta (DAG) I was placed with two unique individuals Mike Hill (Mikey) and Terry Janocha (TJ). Between the two of them they had over fifty years of service with the company. They each had started way back in the day. The stories they would tell me kept me entertained, the day passed quickly. We were all about the same age. Each had children, each took enormous pride in the work we did.

Terry J. was the more serious one. Terry taught me according to the company's established procedures. He would pull the reference and teach from it. With my background in program development, I thoroughly appreciated his approach. Terry was methodical and practical; always available to assist me.

Terry has a dry sense of humor, most people did not fully listen to this wise soul. He always had so much to say.

He did not waste his words, if he perceived someone as not being interested he had few if any words to share with them.

The three of us, Terry, Mike and I, worked in a very small office. We were forever swamped with work, research packages. But just as stress would knock on our door Terry would tell the funniest joke I had ever heard. We would all laugh so hard our stomachs would be aching. Others, including higher management, watched and could not figure it out. Mike and I laughed so hard, we loved Terry's jokes.

Terry is a true family man, his family ALWAYS came first. At one point his wife was relocated out of state by her job. Terry proudly raised his daughter, Amy then a junior in high school. Terry had questions, nonetheless he did an outstanding job as mom and dad. Terry has since retired from Airborne Express.

Terry thank you for teaching me, for caring about me, for sharing all that you had especially your jokes! I still want to take pilot lessons. I Love You.

Mike Hill

I called him Mikey! My friend 'til the end.

Mike's daughter Charity has the same birthday as me. Mike was divorced and very devoted to his two children, Patrick and Charity.

We often talked about the pain he felt, the void in his life caused by his children's absence. I felt Mikey did not have an outlet, somewhere safe where he could just let go.

We would meet often at a nearby sidewalk café and talk for hours. I felt I had known Mike all of my life. That's how we related to each other. Totally open and honest with one another.

Mike was not totally rewarded nor appreciated for his positive contributions to life generally and as a father more specifically.

His children loved him and they spent more time together as they got older, especially Charity. She would keep her father involved with everything going on in her life: from college choice to boyfriends; changing career direction, sharing everything. Their relationship reminded me of how blessed I was to have a similar bond with my father.

And there's that matter that Charity and I shared the same birthday! I met and fellowshipped with Mike's entire family. It did not bother his family at all that his best friend was a black woman. We had so much fun that summer day.

His sister was in town from Hawaii, both of his brothers were there and his Mom.

During our café chats, we would release, verbally, all the concerns with work. We did not want to burden our mates with the details from Airborne. We talked about our Families, and usually ended with our personal goals and dreams.

Literally exchanging our worlds until the café would close its doors, and we would have to leave.

Mikey, I Love You so much. Thanks for a true and honest friendship.

Mike Martin

I came from a management background, well once a manager always a manager.

With the lack of written references to perform several of the functions required, I took on the responsibility. Mike was fully

supportive of my endeavors. Mike agreed to
submit the final version to Corporate to be
used company wide. However Mike was
separated from the company before it was
finished.

Mike opened his own business after leaving.
We remain friends. Mike is never too busy to
talk with me. I appreciate his respect, love
and care for me. I am grateful to Mike for
maintaining his Christian spirit on the job.

Jim Davie

No scenario of male relationships would be
complete without inclusion of my buddy.

Jim managed one of the contractor teams
however he was completely knowledgeable of
Airborne's procedures. Jim taught me a lot
about how to do my job.

Jim was always joking and kidding around;
but never when there was work to do. He
remained a loyal component of Airborne. Jim
would be there without fail. I doubt he ever
missed one single day without having planned
it first. He is an exceptional individual.

Jim's love for jamming on his guitar with
his band was something he always talked
about. He invited folks out to hear his
group all the time, including me. I have yet
to hear him other than a few songs at the
office. He is good; he feels the music in
his very soul. A true musician!

Jim I miss your wit and charm. I pray all
continues to be well in your world.

Greg Dial

My first Supervisor with Airborne, I started as a part time employee.

Although the company's policy was to only promote individuals with a College degree, Greg respectfully submitted my name when a position became available.

During the interview the District Manager advised me again of the policy. Mike Drew then said, "Greg is putting his job on the line. He feels confident in your abilities and qualifications."

I was promoted to Supervisor and transferred each time Greg got reassigned to a different station. We spent four and one half years together before I transferred to a station closer to my home.

Greg had absolute confidence in my ability to get the job done, by whatever means necessary. We were not always in agreement about the best method to use but we remained respectful of the other.

Under Greg's management I supervised first the highest inbound station in Atlanta and I graduated to supervising the third highest outbound station in the Country!

I hardly ever disappointed Greg, sometimes circumstances were just beyond my control or lack of knowledge where to find resources. All in all 99% of the time we were on one accord.

Greg is an avid camper/hiker, enjoys writing and is a fantastic father to his three children, Lorene, Scott and Tricia. Cathy, Greg's wife is an absolute doll.

Greg found his inner peace up on the mountain top. It is his retreat from the hectic work schedule, his regrouping expedition that he rarely ever misses.

Greg is a great boss, he allows his supervisors complete autonomy to get the job done. That's important for an individual's growth and unfoldment.

Thanks Greg for your unquestionable belief in me! You are a fine Manager. I look forward to working with you again, somewhere, somehow!

Mike Drew

Men can be downright vulgar in each others' company. But all the men I have worked for have consistently shown me the utmost respect.

Mike Drew, Airborne Regional Manager, was the District Manager who reluctantly promoted me! (a little humor inserted)

Mike had a reputation of telling people exactly what he wanted, how he wanted it in very explicit details. If the point required more flavor, a few curse words could be heard blaring out of Mike's mouth.

I am not judging his language one way or the other, just simply stating the facts. He got results and that was the main focus.

I sincerely and most appreciatively thank Mike Drew for never, ever allowing curse words to exit his mouth in my presence. I was the only female supervisor in Mike's district.

The others were all accustomed to his colorful language. I was prepared to hear whatever he had to say in whatever way he chose. I thank Mike for always being a true gentleman. Perhaps I helped to bring out his softer side.

Mike grew to have the same confidence that Greg held of me. When he was promoted to Regional Manager I was happy for him. Thanks Mike.

John Rowan

My current District Manager with Airborne.

John is from the old school of management, micro managing every detail. That's his style and its fine with me.

So many people have trouble relating to John. They want him to change to suit their individual taste or style. I accept John completely just as he is now.

John has a tendency to be stern and rigid. Seldom laughed or smiled before I arrived.

My favorite saying is 'It's all good, all the time'. I believe John thought it was a strange saying for a supervisor, especially a supervisor in a fast-paced, ever changing industry as Airborne.

John began to smile and loosen up. And one day things were getting to me and he called my attention to the fact I was NOT smiling!

I then fully realized I had become the light to brighten the day for all.

John has consistently treated me fairly; allowing me privileges not given to others. But I respected John first.

Learned his ways and dealt with him solely from that place of understanding. I was not there to change him like most people before me had attempted to do. There was and is mutual respect between us. John will go the extra step to ensure my contentment and I appreciate him for his display of respect for me.

John you are great just the way you are. I enjoy your smile! Thanks!

My Romantic Escapades

I had abandonment issues buried deep inside my heart. Those issues have affected each of my romantic relationships. Sometimes I held on, refused to let go because I could not bear the thought of being alone.

I was forty five years old when I discovered the beauty within me, that I was excellent company to fellowship with, all by myself.

It came about as a result of leaving my home town, departing from everything that was familiar and routine. I found inner peace sitting on my deck in a wooded area simply communing with nature.

Absent were the sounds of sirens, helicopters and gun fire. It was quiet, so quiet that initially it was difficult for me to fall asleep.

This is not to imply everyone must leave the metropolitan, big city and move south. This is just to say the south is where I discovered my contentment.

The abandonment issues arose from hearing, almost daily, how my father had abandoned his children, his responsibilities.

As a child I took what was said literally. I didn't know it would damage the way I related to men later in my life.

Nor did I ever consider my mother may have had unresolved issues with my father that caused her to talk badly about him.

It was fear that caused my mother and step father to belittle my dad. My mother remained wounded because the relationship between her and my dad had failed.

She needed to justify herself that he was the sole responsible being for their breakup. My step father said the things he did perhaps because he sensed that my mother still had strong feelings for my dad and he needed to diffuse those feelings. I don't believe it was done maliciously but rather as a survival technique for them.

I have come to accept that both my mother and step father did the best they knew how in raising all of us.

I have told them this repeatedly for the last twenty years, after becoming a mother myself. I wonder however if I said it in a way that they understood I held no malice in my heart, I love them the same.

Although I consciously made an effort to forgive them, I had not considered the impact those abandonment issues had on my romantic relationships.

I desperately longed for a man to love me and never leave me. Never fully realizing that when I fully loved myself unconditionally I didn't need to have someone else validate my worthiness.

I didn't need someone else to make me complete! I was whole all by myself. I suppose my desperation weighed heavily on the men who I shared a romantic relationship with. Those desperation feelings can seem suffocating to an unsuspecting soul. Overbearing to the most loving individual.

To recognize my inappropriate behavior had taken time. Time spent in forgiveness of myself and others, for believing in inadequacy.

Time spent in recognizing and fully accepting I am a child of God, therefore I am whole and complete!

Time spent in prayer and meditation seeking the truth of God.

Time spent in releasing all of the past in the most loving way possible.

I emerge whole, happy and healed! I emerge accepting I cannot change the past because it is already done, over. I emerge with a new attitude of LOVE, period!

I choose to acknowledge I am a survivor not a victim!

To the men who loved me intimately. Laughter and wonderment was indeed a great part of our union. I could not have considered loving you otherwise.

To the ones who didn't love themselves and thought suffocating me with their love, placed me atop a pedestal, would somehow make them capable of loving.

To the men I couldn't love in return because somewhere, a long, long time ago I labeled myself un-lovable.

To the men who hurt just as much as I did, we really thought we had it all together.

Each of you know, I pray, that I love and loved you the best way I knew how at the time.

I have had many boyfriends during my life; each one a very unique individual. Yes, I learned valuable lessons from them; Yes I participated in unhealthy relationships. I am enriched emotionally by them also.

I grew through them I believe, I trust that I did anyway.

I will share my adult relationships, two marriages, an admirer, a former finance and my one True Love.

Jeff Tyson

When I first saw Jeff in 1970, immediately I thought he was the most handsome man I had ever met.

As our relationship developed I always found something new to love about this man. He was kind and fine!

He was generous, funny and loved life; genuinely a great person.

Our first encounter took place shortly after his discharge from the Army where he served on active duty in Viet Nam.

I had little or no understanding of the devastating effects this war had on the lives of those that served this, our country. There were more casualties than were reported because many if not all those that survived that horrific experience were casualties!

This veteran's wartime experience was detrimental to him and our life together.

Jeff was surely, deeply wounded by all the deaths and dying he witnessed. A permanent mark had been made, he was emotionally wounded.

How could he not be? He had pictures, if his memory failed him, of his best friends' torn dead bodies. I cannot begin to imagine what that must have felt like. It's difficult viewing a loved ones' whole - intact body in a coffin. But to see pieces is an absolutely different experience totally! And he had terrible nightmares,

I know Jeff loved me, I loved Jeff and we loved each other. So on my twenty first birthday he proposed and I eagerly accepted.

My two best girlfriends were already married by then. So ready or not I was next to walk down the aisle.

My family and friends loved Jeff as much as I did.

Jeff's family was so warm and accepting of me. It was a perfect match. We were all one big happy family.

Our marriage was exciting. Jeff had his own business, a gas/service station. He loved doing mechanical work on vehicles. I loved to watch him work.

Jeff had a motorcycle and we would ride all the time. He has always been gifted with the ability to create a working machine from a broken down piece of junk, scrap metal.

I remember Jeff bringing home a Harley Davidson, I was thinking now that's really nice.

Jeff took his time, he had enormous patience while restoring vehicles. In his mind he designed the finished product. I anxiously awaited the completion. He worked on his bike every chance he got with his sisters' husbands who were all bikers.

The Harley was incredible; he had an exquisite bike by everyone's standards. I was so proud of him, in awe of his abilities. That bike shined like brand new money, chromed down. Fantastic paint job adorned the tank and fenders.

The joy in sharing that experience, of riding as often as possible are forever stamped in my heart.

I would sew us matching outfits to wear. After all, I wanted to contribute to the experience also. Fellow bikers wanted to see what Jeff had done differently to the bike and what I had made for us to wear. It was a joint adventure.

Several years later Jeff purchased an ice cream truck. That's right! Side opening windows and all.

I was shocked but trusted his instincts and ability to transform vehicles. Again his meticulous genius went into high gear. As Jeff completed the mechanical restoration, I remodeled the inside making curtains and seat covers. Another Masterpiece!

Everyone simply called it 'The Ice Cream Truck'. It was so beautiful, a project completed by both of us with love and skill.

We drove the Ice Cream Truck across country, one of the best vacations of my life. Not just because we were driving 'our' machine but also because I was finally pregnant!

Jeff and I had wanted to have children right away after our marriage. It was actually 3 three years later that I conceived. But not without a lot of challenges and false hopes of pregnancy.

Monthly visits to the doctor, me going to specialists and the last option was Jeff going to the fertility clinic. It took a great deal of convincing from me to get him to go. A lot of begging and pleading. I had always dreamed of having a large family – cheaper by the dozen mentality.

Lots of children was my goal. After conceding to we had done everything we could do and without positive results, I reluctantly agreed to relax. Once I did that, stopped focusing all my attention on getting pregnant is when it happened.

One of the greatest moments in my lifetime, was being told by Dr. Hershey that I was pregnant. One of the absolute most ecstatic moments was the birth of our son, Malcolm Jerome Tyson.

After winning the battle of getting pregnant we began the long process of selecting a name. We, I bought books with names. We would say the names, tried to figure out what nickname would be associated and so on.

We had at some time, agreed upon Ezekiel. But was later changed, after birth. Jeff did not want a junior, felt each person must have their own identity. I felt his son should at least have his initials, MJT. Our son was the most beautiful baby in all of St. Mary's Hospital. We were very proud parents.

Jeff often had nightmares about his horrifying experience in Viet Nam. Years later he was still crippled by it. In the end I let Jeff down. Didn't know or understand how to help him deal with his pains. It frightened me to the point of causing separation in our marriage.

He became angry with me probably because I couldn't give him what he needed the most - compassion. I understand that now, today.

Jeff withdrew earlier in our marriage, emotionally. We were both in denial and much pain.

Jeff, I Love You. I appreciate our times together.

Thank You for our beautiful son.

Kevin Lamont Rodgers

I first met or didn't meet Kevin Rodgers at a New Year's Eve party given by me and several of my closest girlfriends.

I say didn't meet because I don't remember our first meeting! I had really gotten into the party spirit, was pretty wasted, had consumed too much alcohol.

So when Kevin called me at home a few days later and said I gave him my telephone number I didn't remember, called him a liar.

Told him he was probably looking over my shoulder when I gave the number to one of my childhood friends. I was very rude to him.

I was not looking to get involved with someone, had just received my divorce from my first marriage. I really cannot then or even now recall giving him my number.

Our friendship began to grow by many telephone conversations we had. Then finally came the time for me to see him for my first time. Keep in mind Kevin knew what I looked like.

Anyway with the gigantic wall around my heart and emotions I was totally NOT interested in anything more than being friends.

Kevin has a very deep and sexy voice. The memory of my one and only blind date took complete control of my senses. This first blind date I had met over the phone. We had arranged for a day time outing. I was anxious, this was something definitely unique for me to do.

This man had a very deep and sexy voice on the phone. I was looking out the window, excited and waiting for my date.

And to my utter amazement, this man drove up in a lime green car, had on a lime green suit and topped it off with a lime green hat! Even back in the earlier times of my young adulthood - LIME GREEN was not chic!

So here I am, faced once again with a man who possessed the deepest, sexiest voice ever. And boy was I dreading this encounter but I had agreed to do it. My only defense was to look as ugly, homely, plain jane as possible.

I searched my closets for the worst looking, baggy outfit. I tied a scarf, a head rag on my head. By all accounts my looks alone would have turned off the most desperate suitor.

Kevin was in shock as I opened the door. We still laugh about that situation. I snatched off the head rag, combed my hair and changed my clothes!

Kevin was fine!

Our friendship grew over the years. We became the best of friends. We shared everything about ourselves. His daughter Toi and my son Malcolm were very close in age.

We had a lot in common. I believe we were best of friends because we were so much alike, mirrored each other. He was handsome and a ladies man, I was pretty and a flirt. We were both physically fit, took good care of our bodies. We each had lots of friends and enjoyed socializing.

The biggest difference between us was Kevin is spontaneous and I prefer order and plans. So we learned to balance, using the others' strength and it was good, an opportunity to grow. Kevin actually had a hard time convincing me to just do something, on the spot simply because I or we wanted to do it. It was fun.

We became intimate because of a dare he made to me. Completely spontaneous, totally unplanned. Kevin was my best friend. But I felt I had to win this one. At first we felt we had made a mistake. As we talked more about the situation, the more we convinced ourselves to start dating.

The majority of our relationship has been filled with fun and laughter, good times. The fact remained we were very close friends. Yes I know and agree married folks must be friends, but our situation was different somehow. We didn't start with that end in our minds.

Just like the dare to be intimate, one day Kevin called and said, "Let's get married. We can go to Vegas today!" I arranged for a babysitter for Malcolm and off we went.

We were eloping! Complete spontaneity.

We laughed the entire three hour ride. Arrived in Vegas, I still could not believe I was doing this. It was extremely exciting and romantic. We searched for a wedding chapel. When we finally found one that we agreed on we stopped. We parked the car, still laughing.

As I closed my car door I got my finger caught in it. It hurt so bad. We treated my finger and headed back to Los Angeles, unmarried.

My family was furious with me, that I had even considered eloping. What was I thinking? Is what I heard over and over again. They didn't understand that was probably the single most exciting adventure I had ever experienced.

So we planned the wedding according to tradition.

We had fun during the entire planning process. We mixed our tastes and it was a grand affair. Identical to our relationship, the wedding ceremony was very unique.

In fact, we were the first black couple to get married at the infamous Crystal Cathedral in California.

Everyone pitched in to help plan this awesome ceremony. My son, Malcolm, then only five years old escorted me down the aisle.

Our family and friends came from across the United States to attend. Finally it was time to depart for our honeymoon. We went first class to the Poconos. The whole everything was filled with so much joy.

Although we tried, we had no children. And soon after the wedding, problems began to surface.

Kevin admits he listened to some well-wishers, some older men from work who warned him the relationship would change, especially me after the ceremony. When things or I did not change, he had to. Strange how much power and influence we give to people who don't know your truth!

Normal everyday actions became a nuisance. We fought to have fun, which was so unlike us.

We broke up in 1985, I filed for divorce and waited out the six months for it to be final. After which I changed my name back.

Several years later, Kevin dropped by to say his mother was not doing so well. I called Mom, Kevin's mother and she told me he was in trouble and needed my help. That was the beginning of our second attempt to be husband and wife.

I had read an article in the newspaper which stated many divorces filed in 1985 were never granted the final dissolution.

Yes, you are right – we were still legally married. We didn't need to remarry, I just had to change my name back to Rodgers. Did we resolve the issues that created the desire for divorce...NO!

Kevin always showered me with gifts. Every Saturday morning I received fresh flowers. Gifts were usually not given for any specific reason, just because he wanted to buy me something.

We spoiled each other with parties, trips – it didn't matter. My 40th birthday, Kevin rented an entire Hotel. All my friends and family came to Palm Springs. The Palm Tee Hotel was ours for the weekend. It was a surprise party orchestrated by Kevin and

Malcolm. Thanks that was so unusually different!

Something remained between us, however that prevented us from completely committing to each other. We went to a Minister for counseling and asked what we needed to do to resolve our issues. We talked and he listened.

The Minister's conclusion 'not all marriages are put together by God'. Kevin and I left agreeing he just didn't understand our relationship. After all we must be meant to be together we kept getting back together.

Back and forth, back and forth, we did that about 10-15 no, probably more than 20 times. Break ups were horrible, changing locks on the doors, calling his father or one of my brothers to come and put him out, being chased in the car. Giving his clothes and a prized antique Cadillac away. Simply awful hurtful things/actions.

In the final analysis . Kevin scared me. He gave so freely, was so spontaneous. And during our many breakups I had hardened my heart, the soft spot where love resides.

There was too much unresolved pain that we refused, because of our stubborn egos, to deal with honestly. Both refusing to be wrong or to even compromise. So at last the divorce which wasn't became a done deal!

I first met Kevin December 31, 1978, 23 years later we have regained our friendship. I can discuss so much with him without judgment or criticism. He now listens to me.

I enjoy Kevin's company, spirit and friendship. He's insightful and can now be completely honest with me again.

I assumed most of the responsibilities of the marriage, denied Kevin his role of provider. I didn't trust him to be mature and accountable to handle things.

Perhaps I felt that way because he is seven years my junior. I felt he spent too much when we went out with our friends, he always picked up the tab. I would be sitting there thinking, but we've got bills to pay.

Kevin greatly resented that, he kept his feelings to himself. Kevin found complete acceptance outside of our marriage. I didn't recognize the signs, I was too busy making sure everything was done in an orderly manner.

This recount was the most difficult to describe. Because although I have remained friends with all of my former lovers, Kevin is the only one that began as my Best Friend.

There's more detail to our story, we perhaps shared more and undoubtedly we currently share at a much deeper level. A lot of time was spent wondering why we couldn't make our marriage work.

I believe we kept going back and forth because we always ended in a hateful attitude. So when the good times resurfaced, we suddenly had amnesia about what needed to be addressed.

Somewhere along the journey I said this relationship must end in love. And when I could finally accomplish that, the temporary high disappeared. And I was able to end the roller coaster ride.

There's lots more I could share but suffice it to say this is a book of healing and not just one relationship.

ULTIMATELY ONLY LOVE RESOLVED OUR ISSUES, RESURRECTED OUR FRIENDSHIP AND HEALED THE WOUNDS!!

Kevin Rodgers, I Love You and keep you and your family in my prayers constantly.

Billy Thompson

As a child, my family spent most summers traveling to Louisiana. The largest portion of my relatives still lived in central Louisiana in the area of LeCompte and Alexandria.

I became infatuated with my best friend's brother Billy Thompson. Those were the awkward years of puberty, when girls just giggled when they saw a boy they thought was 'cute'. I held that interest with Billy for a long time. We lived miles apart so our meetings were always temporary.

Our dads had been classmates together. My brother William and Billy were close friends. So there was some foundation.

Life happened along the way. Billy went into the service, got married and that was that.

In 1993, some thirty years later, Billy came to Los Angeles to find me. Fortunately I was single at the time. That was so romantic! A man would travel such a long distance looking for me.

Our relationship was short lived but an important part of my life. What I had with Billy was my first completely sober romantic experience.

We communicated at a very deep level. Entertaining him was challenging. He didn't drink alcohol or indulge in any unhealthy addiction. Billy taught me how to dig deep to bring out the pure me, un-intoxicated me.

Billy would talk of a future together, but he wouldn't allow me inside his heart. He kept his heart chained up and protected.

I thank Billy for loving me the best way he knew how at the time. I thank him for making me feel so special, even if for a fleeting moment in time.

Jesse Jennings

My friend, fiancée, former fiancée and now _____, I don't know the word to describe what's happening between us now. Perhaps the answer will be revealed by the completion of this book.

Jesse has been diagnosed with and recently undergone surgery for cancer. The doctors say it has spread into the colon and perhaps the liver.

Because of Jesse's love for me I believe he kept his illness a secret. I feel as though he has known for awhile.

Our relationship deteriorated during the process. He has always been such a private, suffering individual. And instead of telling me what was going on with him, he allowed our relationship to end. Or at least the marriage part of it.

I would get so angry with him. Deep inside of me I felt something different was happening. He wouldn't disclose the truth.

Other aspects of our relationship suffered, ending with the finances. I often tell couples who seek my counsel that finances are never the root cause. Finances are more often a symptom rather than the illness itself.

I tell people to search for the underlying, unspoken and unaddressed issues. I never realized I was guilty of not addressing the root cause.

Jesse became a stranger, someone I no longer knew or liked. Perhaps his change was a direct result of him silently thinking about his health issues. He became withdrawn, distant and silent.

I would become frustrated with Jesse because he stopped dreaming about what he wanted to accomplish in his life. He would say often, "All I want is your happiness, for you to fulfill your dreams."

I felt suffocated, a phrase I used to describe my feelings. By the look in his eyes what I said hurt him deeply. Jesse had wonderful goals and aspirations. I wanted him to fulfill his destiny, not live through mine.

But he couldn't, wouldn't and didn't tell me his prognosis. Whenever he went to the doctor, which was becoming more frequent, he would conceal the truth. This was the compassionate demonstration of his unconditional love for me. I did not know, so I refused it, pushed it aside.

Men, I beg you not to withhold vital information from your mate. When truth is not shared, it can be camouflaged to look like something else.

It may rob you of precious moments spent with people who sincerely love you. Jesse told me years ago that he was raised with the undisputable belief men kept their problems to themselves, a man had to figure his own way out of a situation.

I don't fault his father for instilling that value. I am sure that was how he was raised also, He simply passed that code of conduct on to his son, who lived by it faithfully.

Yet, Jesse was hurting inside. He was torn between doing what he had been taught by his loving father and what he actually knew would allow him peace.

Our communication was or had been very open from the beginning. We shared honestly with one another. The dialog remained that way until this crisis occurred.

I began to experience a feeling of rejection and abandonment. Jesse had shut down completely right in front of my face. I could not coerce the truth from him. I would ask and ask and ask.

Perhaps I was forcing him to a position he could not comfortably handle. He kept it a secret until he had surgery.

I love Jesse with all my heart. The type of compassionate love he is demonstrating for me and my well being is awesome.

I want to share this health challenge with him, if he will allow me. Jesse I know God is healing your body, even as I write this. Be well and remain in God's grace and mercy.

My true love….Tolbert.

I know this will come as a shock and surprise to many who are reading this.

You see I did not marry this man, the one who I call my True Love. I have written many poems to him which I will share with you.

I have dreamt of this man for years. No he is not fictional just unavailable. I love him just the same and pray for only happiness in his life and affairs.

These are my first writings about him:

I've tried to make the words rhyme,
But my love for you
Doesn't end sentences with
Words that sound alike.

You're a PLUS – A Positive – An encouragement
With you I've learned making
A mistake isn't the end.
But rather a learning tool,

A stepping stone.

 The Joy
The Happiness
The Smiles
The Laughter
The Fun
Are all just a part.
With You
I am me!
That is itself is saying a lot,
Love is what you're (we're) about.

I would like to compose a song
'specially for you
But……
Composing is not my gift.

I would like to paint your portrait
But…..
Painting is not my gift.

So….

I write to you - Of you
'cause writing is my gift.

You've brought sunshine - a true brightness

Into my life. My mere existence.
You've given me LOVE in so, so

Many unspoken ways.
You've been strength for two

When I was too weak to stand alone.
You are my true LOVE-

My knight in shining armor.

With you I have no fear,

'cause I know you will protect me
against all humanly possible.

I've grown, matured, blossomed
And its all because of you.

I shine like a star

Because I love you
And you are who you are.

With you-

I am part of two.
Two is a pair

When I'm with you

Love is in the air.

Stay forever by my side
If you leave
A part of me
Will surely die.

With words,
With thoughts
With love.

WITH ALL THAT I CAN GIVE TO YOU

YOU BEAUTIFUL BLACK MAN

L O V E !!!!

BE OURS
ETERNALLY.

My creative energy just soared as I shared
my life with this awesome individual. But we
were both injured and had not taken the

necessary time to heal before we started
what we thought was a life together. Years
later we ask each other, what happened? Why
didn't we make it together?

This next piece explains the positive energy
flowing through me, us.

1980

You have touched the lives of many by
touching me.

You have given encouragement through
positive re-enforcement.

When I speak now to friends and family I
pass on what I learned from you.

It don't cost nothing to smile-

Bury the negative-
At no cost sell yourself to be what others
vision you should be-

Life's too short to waste, even a single
moment - LIVE IT UP.

I thank you for taking the time.

All too often we lose sight of our Blackness
- Our Dignity - Our Pride.

You have gone deep inside of me to find a
person I never knew existed.

Through your strength I've gained security.

Witnessing your joy - I can smile.
Your sincerity has given me strength.

Positive thinking breeds power.

The meaning?
The message?

C'mon Black Folks –
All we need do
Is try!!

This was written after the breakup.

As I sit

I reminisce
Bourbon on ice
Music fills the air
I'm lonely
But I've forced (chased)
Everyone out of
My life
Why?

Didn't I realize that
Someday
Someday – I'd be lonely
And in need
Of companionship-
For the moment
I'm thinking
But will I think
Again
Before I run off the
Next person?

That someday
When the rain
Is pouring
And

I'm in the mood
For solitude
With that special

Someone
I'll be lonely
Again

And…..

I have loved
Truly loved
Only twice in my life
I'm separated (by choice)
From both
But I need
One of them——-
The first will never be
Again
But the second
Well……

Hell - I'm going to try
To mend the break
I want to love and
Be loved.
I'm afraid
Afraid to let myself
Go——

I don't want to hurt
Not like the first time

But…..

I'm hurting now
Because
I LET LOVE PASS ME BY——
WHY?????

Reading these love poems one would only
wonder what happened to this pair. Well LOVE
is what didn't happen. We were both hurting
and too stubborn to say it, to confess it.

Was fear of vulnerability the cause, perhaps we will never truly know.

It's strange the love has never left me. I keep looking for it in every man I meet. Tolbert remains my true love for now what must be 20+ years.

Cannot determine the exact date we met or even started on this love affair, because it always seemed as if it would last forever.

So there was no need to calculate a date to celebrate, anniversaries to remember. Always is forever and that was the only thing to remember.

When we first met, by introduction of my oldest brother George, we were instantly friends. I would be the lone female playing racquetball with two of my brothers and Tolbert.

Those three took no mercy on me. If I wanted to play with them it meant I would thrown against the walls attempting to hit the ball. It meant landing on the ground because I was too slow at hitting the ball. I loved playing racquetball with them.

With all the pain, it was pure fun. The bruises and scraps were simply the price I had to pay to play with them. No harm, No foul.

In those days we were not involved with each other, we were simply friends. And became good friends.

Tolbert showed me a life I never experienced before.

He took me to all the finest restaurants, I ate meals I had never heard the names before. I remember eating Oysters for the very first time. I laugh about it now but it certainly was not funny then.

I remember being taken by limousine to the best area in Los Angeles up on top of a hill, where we were the only customers there. I still believe Tolbert arranged to have it that way, the restaurant was much too lavish not to have other customers.

I was treated like a Queen in every aspect, a tremendous amount of respect always shown to me. Star the rule of the day with him.

Tolbert had a keen sense of style, exquisite taste and a manner about him like no man I had ever met before. I enjoyed every minute we spent together.

We never ever fought, we always lifted each other up to a new and higher level of hope. We always had each other's back. We were always there for each other until the time came for us to display our unconditional acceptance of each other, our flaws were revealed.

We were too strong people, never wanting to admit we hurt, so badly that we just could not bear the pain. We were so stubborn, that even if we were asked, confronted with that pain we would have to deny it unequivocally!

Good or bad it happened to us. But along the way we had found true love that can and will never die. These words of admiration I use to describe my relationship with Tolbert has not come easily to admit.

Just recently I was asked by a very dear friend have I ever truly been in love before.

Before I could cancel the name, Tolbert came flying out of my mouth, to my surprise.
But don't be fooled by me, I really have known this since the end of our relationship some many, many years ago.

It just sounds good to think I had forgotten. Yes I do have a sense of humor. It has served me well in dealing with my past. I thank God for understanding, life is not and was not intended to be so doggone serious!

Tolbert wherever you are presently, I love you. This is not meant to disrespect him in any way. Love is Love. I thank you for allowing me a portion of your life that we shared together.

You really are very special, especially to me. Thanks for sharing that special place within you, that only I saw. You showed me what true love looks and feels like and for that I will always be thankful.

In The End

In the process of thinking and subsequently summarizing my memories of my relationships with the men mentioned in this book healing occurred within me.

I was forced to visit and reconcile some, often very deep, pains and wounds from my past. I also uncovered many truths about situations that I had chosen to deny.

In offering healing to the readers I discovered sincere healing for myself.

The aches and pains, the betrayals and abandonment had weighed me down for years. Brought me down to my knees pleading with God for salvation.

As I remained in a state of pure forgiveness, issues came up. I fully felt the associated pains. I chose to release them completely.

I emerge a person amply capable of fully loving each man in my experience - past, present and future.

This endeavor has been a powerful calling! One that I attempted to ignore.

One that I felt incapable of handling successfully. Doubted I knew the right words to describe a personal journey which we must each take, if we choose to live in LOVE.

Everything unfolds and reveals itself in perfect, absolute, divine time.

I am eternally grateful to myself, for myself, for allowing SPIRIT to guide and direct me through this major process.

For allowing LOVE to heal the wounds and mend the broken places in my heart and soul.

Dear God,

I thank you for using me as the vessel to convey this much needed written account of healing through the most powerful force in the Universe – LOVE.

At times it was difficult to explore some of the relationships. Oh how I did not want to remember or forgive and release. It seemed easier to hold on to the pains.
Actually it has been easier to release them. To accept and know that these men did the best they knew how at the time.

Oh God I pray this book can serve as a tool for others' healing and awakening.

Thanks God for providing me with the most meaningful words to illustrate my experiences. The words flowed so smoothly from my heart and head to paper. God I thank you for this awesome opportunity.

In conclusion, I say thank you to each of you who have taken this journey with me as I share the LOVE shared with me by so many men, especially our Black Men.

The title was not meant to be deceptive, all the men in this book I considered at one time or another to be My Man, hence All My Men is an appropriate title.

This journey would not have been possible to share had it not been for my relentless pursuit of the truth in each of these men.

At times, I was not able or capable of loving them. At other times I was not able to receive their love.

More than not there were times I hurt so bad loving someone was impossible because I lacked the love of myself. I apologize that in my quest to prove something either to another person or myself I injured you along the way.

I never intended to cause harm or injury, please believe and accept my apology. If you have been shocked by some of my revelations, trust me its okay. It took me a long time to accept it as well.

I only want to depart LOVE and its healing affect to everyone I know and those who I don't. We must actively seek to address this issue of unconditional love and make it real for each of us in our pursuit of happiness.

We must love people for who they are, not what we hope them to be or attempt to change them into being. The man, if its you or the one you love, is perfect just the way they are. Learn to love from that vantage point and see miracles happen in your life, right before your very eyes.

I hope this sharing has made healing possible for you.

It makes no difference if you are man or woman, black or white, employed or not. My purpose in this writing was to take a different look at life and love.

Unconditional love is available to all of us who are earnestly seeking it. We need only look through the eyes of love to find it.

In addition to the men named in this book, I remember these men with LOVE and I want to honor their contributions to my life.

A.J. Valentine
Aaron Ali
Ab Karriem
Abdru-Rauf
Al Bacon
Al Jackson
Alamonte Moseley
Alan Smith
Alec Ragsdale
Alfred Lewis
Ali Harris
Allen
Alonzo Jackson
Alonzo Prater
Amin Shakeer
Andre Dyer
Andre Powell
Andrew Theus
Andrew Thomas
Anmer Sumertin
Anthony Toles
Antoine Williams
Arn St. Cyr
Arnold Jackson
Art Jackson
Arthur Broome
Atty. Donald Edwards
Aziz Farrar
Bernard
Bernard Keys
Big Melton
Big Rob
Big Will
Big Will Henderson
Bill Butler
Bill Davis
Bill Gray

Billy Brice
Billy Calcote
Billy Jackson
Bishop Morrow
Bob Caldwell
Bobby Jones
Brad
Brennan Brown
Brent Ford
Brother James
Bruce
Bruce Armstead
Bruce Bowers
Brutus - Glenn Joseph
Buddy Lester
Butch - Marion Martin
Byron Jackson
Byron Nelson
Calvin Jordan
Carl Washington
Carter Townsend
Carvin D. Cade
Cecil Swepson
Champ-Jerry Toles
Charles B. Cotton Sr.
Charles Saunders
Charles Smith
Chief William Jennings
Chip Rudell
Chris Coleman
Chris Jennings
Chris King
Chris O'Quinn
Chub - Allen Wilcher
Clarence Goff
Clarence Howard
Cleveland Deal
Cleveland Johnson
Clinton Goff
Cornelius
Craig
Craig Dunbar

Curley Kinchen
Curtis
D.K.
D'Morris Webb
Dameion Smith
Damon Wright
Daniel McFadden
Danny Wright
Darnell
Darrell Crooks
Darren Elijah
Darren Ringo
Darryl Lee
Darryl Stansell
Darryl Williams
David Fairbanks
David Gistarb Jr.
David Mc Donald
David Toulson
Davon Smith
Davon Wright
Demond Morris
Derrick Brown
Derrick Harrell
Devlin Evans
Dexter Jackson
Don Bush
Don Harris
Donald Ray Cyriark
Donley Minor
Doug Edwards
Doug Tye
Douglas Tejada
Dousaine
Dr. H. L. Worrell
Dr. Kofi Kondwani
Dr. Na'im Akbar
Dr. Sharonde Wilson
Dr. Tiy-E Muhammad
Dwayne Dickey
Dwayne Quander
E.J. Dennis

Earl Allen
Earl Robinson
Earl Rodgers
Ed Banyard
Ed Romero
Eddie Johnson
Edward Carney
Elmo Woods
Eric Ash
Eric Jackson
Felton Perry
Frances
Frank
Frank Akore
Frank Martin
Fred Ferguson
Fred Melton
Fred Stevens
Gabriel Morgan
Gary Adams
Gary Patten
Gary Sharpe
Gentleman Jim McFarland
George Calcote
George E. Hart
George Jackson
Glenn Glass
Glenn Okimura
Grant Cole
Graylen Waltress
Greg Bailey
Greg Provenzano
Greg Rodgers
Gregory McCall
Guniel Lott
Guy Jackson
Hardrick Jennings
Harvey
Herbert Bentz
Herschel Brown
Howard Carter
Hugh Whalum

Idrissa Toure
Imam Ron Al-Amin
Irvin White
Isaac Blazer
Isaac Riggins
J. C. Barmore
J.D Sullivan
Jacob Mikels
Jacolby Williams
Jamar Hamilton
James
James Brown
James Talley
James Williams
Jamey Williams
Jasen Nowak
Jason Hamilton
Jason Patton
Jason White
Jason Williams
Jeff Antonio Daniels
Jeff Coulter
Jeff Daniels
Jermaine Cromantie
Jerome Powell
Jerry Clegg
Jerry Goff Jr.
Jerry Skinner
Jesse Jennings Sr.
Jesse Wilson
Jim Duvall
Jim Hawkins
Jim Kainz
Jim Tate
Jimmy Dismuke
Jimmy Hamilton
Jimmy Morris
Jimmy Rouse
Joe Lyons
John - Hai Tran
John Bolden
John Crayton

John Espana
John Goodkey
Johnnie Wilson
Johnny Williams
Jon Chisholm
Jonathan Slocomb
Jonathan Weston
Joseph White
Juan Cepeda
Judson Powell
Justin Goff
Justin Meinhart
Kadar
Keith Nelson
Ken Baker
Ken Harrison
Kendall Mc Carthy
Kenneth Goethe
Kenneth Nowling
Kennon Goff
Kenny Williams
Kermit Glenn
Kerry Senior
Kevin Tucker
Kinney
Kivon Lindley
L.A. J
LaMar Anderson
Larry Jackson
Larry Morgan
Larry Moseley
Larry Raskins
Larry Worrell
Lawson Washington
Leonard
Leonard Tate
Leslie Franklin
Leslie Smith
Levy Miller
Lindsey
Little Paul
Litton Jones

Lloyd Goff Jr.
Lou Brooks
Major L. Warner
Malcolm Pope
Malik Saleem
Manual Perez
Marcus Davis
Marcus Tyson
Mark Carr
Mark McClain
Mark Rogers
Marlin Carter
Marlon Smalls
Marvin Davis
Marvin Hall
Matt Dearing
Matt Dixon
Maurice Studivant
Maurice Washington
Melvin Kemp
Melvin McKissic
Michael Anderson
Michael Baldwin
Michael Beckford
Michael Espana
Michael Jamerson
Michael Parker
Mike Cupisz
Mike Fath
Mike Galloway
Mike Krach
Mike Sarver
Mike Woodward
Montisse Howell
Montrel Jackson
Mr. Edwin Thomas
Mr. Goodloe
Mr. Groove
Mr. T - Thomas Lovelace
Napoleon Moulder
Nashid Abdullah
Nate

Nazim
Neto Morgan
Nigel Perkins
Noah Purifoy
Northup Hood
Otis Skinner
PaPa Joe Sanders
Pat
Patrick
Patrick Patterson
Paul Cormier
Pepper-Anthony Bowie
Peter York
Phil Maxwell
Phil Sykes
Prof. Joseph Bell
Quincy Beaver
R. V. Thomas
Rafeeq Madyun
Rags Scanlan
Ralph Kilondu
Ralph Sutherland
Randolph
Randy Baker
Ray Cox
Ray-Harden Raiford
Red - Lee McCullough
Rev. Don Everett
Rev. James Edner
Rev. Richard W. Brown
Rev. Robert Kilgore
Rev. Ron Brown
Rev. Terry Winemiller
Rev. Walter Kimbrough
Rev. Willie McDaniel
Ricci Donati
Richard Smith
Richard Townsend
Rick Walters
Robbie Coleman
Robert Burgess
Robert Johnson

Robert Mason
Robert Njoroge
Robert Toomer
Rodney Jackson
Rodney James
Rodney Rowe
Roland Jackson
Ron Carter
Ron Thrower
Ronald Lewis
Ronald Riley
Ronnie Smith
Roosevelt Deal
Roy Robinson
Rudy Goodwine
Rusty Cooper
Sam Anderson
Sam Loner
Sam Teasley
Sean Hawkins
Sean Haynes
Shelly Garrett
Sights
Sir Walter
Spain
Steve Bell
Sylvester
T.G. Cody
Tavares Holloway
Ted Dirkschneider
Ted Myers
Terone Harris
Terry Tyler
Thomas - TIF
Thomas Cryer
Thomas Meeks
Thomas Taylor
Tiger
Tim Washington
Tinsley Allgood
Todd White
Tolliver Mc Kinney

Tom Brussard
Tom Downey
Tommie Walker
Tommy Johnson
Tommy Phillips
Tommy Tighe
Tony Cupisz
Tony Gober
Tony Hill
Tony Murphy
Tony Rodgers
Toons
Touché
Tracy Dixon
Troy Taylor
Twin
Tyke Tyler
Ulises Carranza
Uncle Alonzo Toles
Uncle Bill Brown
Uncle Bobby
Uncle Charlie Armstead
Uncle Clarence
Uncle Moochie
Uncle Pap Brown
Uncle Percy Calcote
Uncle Reed
Uncle Richard Goff
Uncle T.L. Brown
Uncle Versie Brown
Vernon
Vernoy Hite
Victor Martin
Vince Stewart
Wallace Scott
Walter Henderson
Walter Scott
Warren Green
Waymon
Wes Boozer
West
Will Hardy

Will Jones
Will Kelbaugh
William Delaney
William Pitts
William Robinson
Wilson Crawford
X.L. Smith
Youngs Lef

REMEMBERING - FORGIVING - LOVING

Presenter: Sandy Rodgers, author
"All My Men".

This workshop focuses on helping
participants to uncover the pains of the
past that block them from moving forward.

Guides each person towards the forgiveness
journey which ultimately frees a person to
be fully capable of loving unconditionally -
both themselves and others.

Sandy believes self love is a strong
motivator for getting a person's life back
on track. In Sandy's book entitled "ALL MY
MEN," she writes "when love is the key
element in human relationships and
interactions, a better society erupts with
such force that all of our social ills are
completely destroyed!"

Sandy has appeared on radio station KKDA -
Speak Out America in Ft. Worth, Texas;
participated as a speaker at Masjiid Hassan
- Ft Worth, Texas; Marietta Chapel A.M.E.
- Marietta, Georgia; Black Bookworm
Bookstore - Ft. Worth, Texas; Positive Pages
Bookstore - Los Angeles, California;
Southwest Los Angeles College - Los Angeles,
California promoting "ALL MY MEN". Sandy was
the 'Motivational Speaker' at the 2003
National Association of Black Narcotic
Agents' Annual Training in Atlanta, Georgia.

Sandy is available for bookings and enjoys
sharing with others, especially 'men', she
says that's where the largest opportunity
for growth lies. Our men are raised to
believe they are not supposed to cry or show

any emotions, keep everything hid or they
become less of a 'man', so much nonsense
plagues our men. Its time for healing,
period.

Sandy Rodgers
P.O. Box 67
Austell, GA 30168

www.ingramcontent.com/pod-product-compliance
Lightning Source LLC
Chambersburg PA
CBHW062210270326
41930CB00009B/1697